Meditation

The joy of spiritual self knowledge through Sahaja Yoga
meditation

It is not the strongest of the species that survives, nor the most intelligent, but the most responsive to change. Charles Darwin (1809-1882)

MEDITATION

ISBN 0 9548519 0 0

First published 2005 by
Corvalis Publishing
London
www.corvalis.co.uk

MEDITATION

by

Nigel Powell

- CONTENTS -

Dedicated to all seekers of truth

This book is a label attached to the medicine bottle of Yoga. By all means read the label, but do remember that one cannot achieve wellness without taking the medicine itself. Without meditation, these words are no more than scribbles on a page.

The Author

Nigel Powell is a columnist and feature writer for The Sunday Times newspaper in London and is the author of the Sunday Times Book of Computer Answers published by Harper Collins. He has taught and organised yoga meditation classes and seminars around the world for over a decade, and is a regular supporter of community programmes run by the Sahaja Yoga charitable trust in the UK.

- FORWARD -

Sahaja Yoga was founded by Shri Mataji Nirmala Devi in AD 1970.

Nirmala Salve was born at midday on 21st March 1923 in a small town called Chindwara, located close to the geographical centre of India. The birth was unremarkable save for the fact that it was relatively effortless and that the baby was spotless when she arrived, a fact which prompted her name of Nirmala (literally meaning immaculate). Her Christian parents were prominent members of an old dynastic family of the region, and as such were well respected in the local community. Her father practiced as a lawyer and was eventually to become the only Christian member elected to the Legislative Assembly prior to India's independence. His wife was one of the first ladies in India ever to graduate in Mathematics.

Nirmala very quickly established a reputation as something of a special child. Always smiling and playful, she seemed to lead a self possessed and untroubled life in every way. In his book My Memoirs, her late brother H.P. Salve recounts a strange series of unexplained events which occurred during her early life which seemed to point to some special qualities. These include the time when a horse and buggy in which the baby girl was placed careered off at high speed without the driver, stopping only once it had reached the family home.

At the time it was considered something of a miracle that no harm befell the baby during the wild journey, and people were amazed that the strange horse stopped exactly outside the gates with no prompting.

The child grew up in the time of increasing conflict between the old colonial British powers and the burgeoning movement for

Indian independence led by Mahatma Ghandi. Indeed it was during this period that the young girl was invited to spend some time at the great Mahatma's ashram at Wardha during her school vacations, and he made it clear that he was very impressed with her obvious depth and spiritual knowledge. After her schooling Nirmala moved on to study medicine, but was forced to abandon her studies because of her active involvement in the independence movement.

In 1948 she married Mr C. P. (later Sir C. P.) Srivastava, who was to go on to become the longest serving and most decorated Secretary General in the history of the International Maritime Organisation of the United Nations.

However it was not until several decades later, after she had married and raised two daughters of her own, that Nirmala felt she could turn her full attention to her spiritual destiny. So it was that after years of long contemplation on the plight of humanity, and a growing unease with the distortion of spiritual messages being peddled by the so-called gurus of the time, on 5th May 1970 in a place called Nargol in the state of Gujarat, India, Shri Mataji Nirmala Devi manifested her full spiritual powers after a profound night of meditation on a deserted sea shore.

This awe inspiring and momentous event was both the catalyst and the genesis for the evolutionary process of Kundalini awakening that was to follow. It was the birth of Sahaja Yoga and the true beginning of the transformation of humanity from Homo Sapien to Homo Spiritus. Through the power of her meditation she was able not only to effect the opening of her own Sahasrara Chakra, the ultimate spiritual centre necessary for the actualisation of an individual's true yoga, but to replicate this event on a Cosmic plane.

By so doing, by enabling this catalytic unfolding of the primordial Sahasrara, Shri Mataji finally opened the gateway to spiritual mass enlightenment, to a yoga which can be effortlessly experienced by anyone with a genuine desire for spiritual growth.

12

Her destiny fulfilled and her powers now fully manifested, it was not long before she took the opportunity to begin emancipating the world. Slowly at first, but with increasing frequency, news of her spiritual power started to spread to those who were in need. She began to minister to friends and acquaintances, offering them spiritual advice and in certain cases offering spiritual treatments for their illness. It was only when one lady, a Mrs Oak, actually started to accept her teachings as from a Guru sometime in July of 1970, that it could really be said that Sahaja Yoga started in earnest.

Today Sahaja Yoga is practised in over 90 countries of the world. Hundreds of thousands of people have discovered that there is a real spiritual alternative to the apparent chaos of the world, and that real peace can be found through the dedicated practice of this most powerful of yoga meditations. Shri Mataji is still devoted to spreading the benefits of this wonderful process as widely as possible, and she travels the world tirelessly teaching and promoting the truth about spirituality to whoever is prepared to listen with an open heart.

Sahaja Yoga classes are always provided free of charge. Right from the earliest days Shri Mataji made it clear that this ancient knowledge and the process of Divine union through self-realisation is the birthright of every human being, and therefore cannot be charged for.

Classes are organised and run by volunteers who have been impelled by the positive changes in their own lives to pass the gift on to others. These individuals come from all walks of life and occupations, but the single link between them all is their open hearted compassion and genuine desire to help others benefit as they have done. The hire of rooms and payment for materials is also all done through the sincere generosity of these people.

By the same token there is no Sahaja Yoga organisation which one can 'join'.

– INTRODUCTION –

Only the spiritually naïve spend their lives looking merely for comfort and happiness. Anonymous

The purpose of this book is to introduce the reader to the main principles involved in the practice of the Sahaja Yoga technique, and to explain in greater detail how to make the most of the process. It is not intended as an exhaustive guide, nor should it be taken as a definitive pointer to all aspects of yoga, as the subject matter is much too vast to be covered in one small volume.

Hopefully the book will provide enough of an understanding of the major points to lay the groundwork for the reader's own meditation at home. The book is not in any way intended to act as a substitute for a proper course of instruction in the meditation, nor should it be treated as a short cut to becoming a fully spiritual being.

In fact without undergoing the actual process of self realisation, this book may prove to be of little value, and for this reason a simple procedure for attaining self realisation is included at the back of the book under Appendix C. Again the reader is urged not to use this as a way to avoid undertaking a properly structured course in this amazing yoga meditation, but more as a simple primer to the procedure and practice of Sahaja Yoga.

A list of Sahaja Yoga websites around the world is contained in Appendix E to help interested readers locate their nearest centre and take advantage of further free tuition.

– CHAPTER ONE –

If you want to improve, be content to be thought foolish and stupid with regard to external things. Epictetus, The Enchiridion

THE NATURE OF REALITY

We take it for granted that we live in the real world, and rely on many different facts to prove it. For one thing, our world is reassuringly solid to touch, and we can see, hear, smell and taste an abundant range of things which make our reality substantial. We are alive.

But despite this seemingly simple observation, we continue to remain chronically uninformed about the true nature of our universe, both external and internal. Scientists continually conduct experiments and formulate hypotheses about the material universe, while eminent philosophers offer their own view of the nature of being, but still we cannot answer the simplest of questions – why are we here and what is the reality of consciousness?

These are not new questions, they have been puzzling the deep thinkers of the world since the dawn of civilisation, but even today, thousands of years later, it is almost impossible to find clear answers.

Much of the reason for this failure to make sense of our universe lies in the fact that our consciousness is constrained by the limits of our mind. This mind, with its prejudices, inadequate education and limited imagination is, by and large, stuck in a rut of narrow mental boundaries. It's not just that we don't know the answers, it's more that we cannot even imagine what questions to ask. And so we make guesses, using our imagination, previous wisdom and a dash of wild sauce to add flavour.

I believe that...the world of our daily experience - the world of tables, chairs, stars and people, with their attendant shapes, smells, feels and sounds - is a species-specific user interface to a realm far more complex, a realm whose essential character is conscious. It is unlikely that the contents of our interface in any way resemble that realm... if consciousness is fundamental, then we should not be surprised that, despite centuries of effort by the most brilliant of minds, there is as yet no physicalist theory of consciousness, no theory that explains how mindless matter or energy or fields could be, or cause, conscious experience. [i]

On the one hand there are the rationalists and scientists who scoff at the improvable nature of spiritual issues and so focus on the measurable mechanics, whilst on the other, dedicated followers of the ethereal insist that science is missing the point completely. Both sides are unfortunately limited by identical trappings of mind and ego, and so are doomed to argue for eternity.

But there is another way. A method which has been in use for thousands and thousands of years by ancients and wise men across the world. It is called yoga, and it is the method of taking our consciousness beyond the constraints of the mind and into a new dimension. We literally – in that time honoured cliché – become one with the universe.

We have to transcend the mind, in order to address our deepest questions in a way which is not limited by constricted mental logic – we need in effect to 'become' the answers. In this way we can have absolute knowledge within ourselves which does not suffer from educational flaws or earthbound misconceptions, and we can know absolutely the truth of our perception.

The ancient Seers quickly learned the truth of this, and over time developed a pattern of contemplation which seemed to flood them with insights into the human condition. These insights were strong enough to withstand the repeated scrutiny of enquiring minds, and deliver the kind of answers which clearly were rooted in the truth. These introspections were also linked to visions and preternatural experiences, and because they were replicated simultaneously across vast geographical distances by a variety of unconnected people, they slowly came to be acknowledged as divine revelations of cosmic knowledge, delivered to humanity via an invisible and yet ever present consciousness. It was the beginning of man's true spiritual communication.

THE UNIVERSAL SPIRIT

When we talk of the consciousness of the universe, we of course dive into areas which are impossible to prove and even harder to explain. Ancient civilisations clearly had a very pragmatic view of this relationship between man and his universe, attaching simple icons such as the Earth Mother to the concept of a divine architect, but in almost every case they also tacitly showed deference to a universal spirit which governed the crops, seasons and laws of nature as well as the overall health and happiness of the people.

This view – or some would say understanding – of the nature of the universe reigned unchallenged for thousands of years, only gradually losing ground as the transition to a scientifically focussed civilisation took root in the West and beyond, so that the role of God and the spiritual universe began to take a back seat in our belief system.

Nevertheless, there are those who believe that we will eventually be forced to return to a more holistic understanding of our existence if we ever hope to provide answers to the ultimate questions of how and why. Science and rationality, it seems, can only help us understand the mechanical issues.

The ancient spiritual teachings suggest that we all come from one source, from that single infinite and timeless consciousness that is the sum total of everything that exists. We can call this Oneness, this consciousness, whatever we like, but it has the unique quality of being unknowable through the mind. It can only be known through experience, through the light of inner experience reflected on our emotional and mental makeup.

17

This One is in effect everything that is NOT, a negation of everything that is, or that is knowable in our ordinary sphere of existence. This Not-ness cannot be described, as it has no earthly counterpart, no imagery with which to give it form. In the same way, we can never 'know' it, as there is no mental concept which can give it a place in our imaginings.

There is no space involved in this definition, no sense of time, of beginning or end. It just is. We can only say, perhaps, that the Not-ness has interfaces through which we may 'experience' a fraction of its being. These interfaces, which we can think of as different states of being, let us 'perceive' the One via a combination of feeling, emotion and direct subtle experience which are a form of reality we can handle.

The ancient Seers called this process of perception 'realisation', to emphasise its core experiential quality, something beyond mere mental thought. And so we can 'realise' that which is not, through experiencing it as love or joy, both of which in their purest form are nothing more than the manifestation of a Divine state of being. In the same way we can also sense a crude approximation of the void of consciousness by experiencing the peace, the silence of God in meditation.

And so the ancients determined through deep introspection and vision the essence of that which is unknowable; and having achieved this weak but precious facsimile of the ultimate, sought to give it some meaning. Of course there is no real meaning that can be given to something so utterly alien to our simple minds, and they were left with the very merest outline of That which Is, and is Not. This clumsy interpretation is what the ancients defined as Sat, Chit, Ananda - Truth, Consciousness, Bliss.

Despite the difficulty of describing this unknowable state, we can share a little of their experiences through some of the powerful writings they have left us down the ages.

Om. I am neither the mind, Intelligence, ego, nor chitta,
Neither the ears, nor the tongue, not the senses of smell and sight,
Neither ether, nor air.
I am Eternal Bliss and Awareness.
I am Shiva! I am Shiva!

I am neither the prana, nor the five vital breaths,
Neither the seven elements of the body, nor its five sheaths,
Nor hands, nor feet, nor tongue, nor other organs of action.
I am Eternal Bliss and Awareness.
I am Shiva! I am Shiva!

Neither fear, greed nor delusion, loathing nor liking have I,
Nothing of pride, of ego, of dharma or liberation,
Neither desire of the mind, nor objects for its desiring.
I am Eternal Bliss and Awareness.
I am Shiva! I am Shiva!

Nothing of pleasure and pain, of virtue and vice do I know,
Of mantra, of sacred place, of Vedas and sacrifice,
Neither I am the eater, the food or the act of eating.
I am Eternal Bliss and Awareness.
I am Shiva! I am Shiva!
Death or fear, I have none, nor any distinction of caste,
Neither father nor mother, nor even a birth, have I
Neither friend nor comrade, neither disciple or Guru
I am Eternal Bliss and Awareness.
I am Shiva! I am Shiva!

I have no form or fancy,
The All-Pervading am I,
Everywhere I exist,
And yet I am beyond the senses,
Neither salvation am I , nor anything to be known.
I am Eternal Bliss and Awareness.
I am Shiva! I am Shiva!
Tad Niskala by Shri Adi Sankaracharya (788-820 AD)

The early Risis, or wise men, who touched these experiences of realisation, did so with a sense of reverence and wonder. They had caressed the very fabric of existence and were properly deferential to the awe inspiring nature of their discovery. They learned through meditation, which served as their communication channel with this benign power, that the all pervading consciousness – the Paramatma or Brahman – split into two to create the Universe. This split, into a figurative male and female aspect, created the matter within which we exist, the beings which inhabit the material universe and the alternate universes which house the purely spiritual aspects of being.

In their understanding, this consciousness also created the many different energies that pervade the universes, including those which were specifically produced to represent the human form, spiritual and physical. Each individual human being was composed of a tiny drop or reflection of the infinite male consciousness called the Jivatman, which, combined together with a tiny drop of the female aspect known as the Kundalini, made up the individual Soul.

According to the ancients a complex tapestry of both subtle and primordial elements were modelled into the material world to sheathe the Soul and give consciousness to the individual through the formation of mind. Within this mind were the ego and super ego, themselves tiny reflections of Cosmic versions, whose purpose was to fuel the creation and the continual cycle of birth and death – Samsara - which is the wheel of existence. This in turn fuelled our Karmas, from the Sanskrit word meaning 'deed', by which every action or motive of ours has a consequence which will come to fruition either in this life or a future one. If we are good the consequence is positive, if we are bad, they will be negative.

The Karmas created by this perpetual cycle of existence in turn powered the evolution of the universe, whilst at the heart of the whole play was a process of evolution in which the individual moved slowly from a state of sleepy ignorance to full and glorious self knowledge. At this point they became aware of their real nature and rejoined the universal consciousness through the merging of their separate subtle energies into the One infinite ocean.

And this material universe, the backdrop to the whole primordial play, was to act as nothing more than a source of instruction, to help the jivatman return to their rightful state of awareness. Through the duality and choice of good versus evil, right vs. wrong, materialism vs. spirituality and a billion other alternatives faced in their freedom of choice by individuals throughout their lives, the play of human evolution could be spun out.

So it was that the practise of yoga was introduced, delivered to humanity through inspired meditation, and perhaps also via the work of fully realised messengers who took birth to bring the Divine secrets to the enquiring minds of the world. Whatever the form, its purpose was to lead the seeker towards the one and only ultimate truth.

THE ROLE OF YOGA IN DEFINING REALITY

In the beginning there was That. In deep peace.

Neither being or not being, neither death or not death, all in an indistinguishable ocean of darkness in darkness.

And desire came upon That which breathed without breath, and through this was the first seed of soul formed. There was a bond formed between existence and non existence, a union created.

And so were seeds planted and powers formed. And love created from below and from above.

Perhaps it was above, perhaps it was below. Who knows the Truth?

Who can then say from where and how this creation came? The Gods came after, so who knows therefore from whence it has arisen?

Whether it was made or not, or from where it came or not, only That in the highest knows. Or maybe does not.

Rig-Veda X.129.4-6. The Creation Hymn

The ancient knowledge that delivered this powerful poem on the puzzle of reality, also presents an intricate explanation of the nature of life and the universe. One that has been resilient enough to withstand the test of thousands of years, and the onslaught of a deeply scientific epoch. It is interesting to note that despite the fact that man's knowledge of material science has progressed beyond all imagination, some of the most eminent scientists in their fields have continued to acknowledge that we may all be subject to some overall creative agency of which we know nothing. Professor Albert Einsten, one of the greatest intellects of the 20th century put it plainly;

'My religion consists of a humble admiration of the illimitable superior Spirit who reveals himself in the slight details we are able to perceive with our frail and feeble minds. The deeply emotional conviction of the presence of a superior reasoning Power, which is revealed in the incomprehensible universe, forms my idea of God'[ii]

Dr Erwin Schrödinger, Nobel prize winner and a founding father of modern quantum science, also showed an appreciation of the fact that science could never provide all of the answers to life.

'I'm very astonished that the scientific picture of the real world is very deficient. It gives a lot of factual information, puts all our experience in a magnificently consistent order, but it is ghastly silent about all and sundry that is really near to our heart, that really matters to us. It cannot tell a word about red and blue, bitter and sweet, physical pain and physical delight, knows nothing of beautiful and ugly, good or bad, God and eternity. Science sometimes pretends to answer questions in these domains, but the answers are very often so silly that we are not inclined to take them seriously.'[iii]

The current convergent middle ground is held today by the Intelligent Design theorists, who believe that certain features of the universe and living things can only be explained by an intelligent cause – a sort of cosmic designer. Arguments continue to rage over the definition and scope of this new religion–science, just as in the past atheists and believers locked horns.

The result of these cumulative efforts to investigate the cell—to investigate life at the molecular level—is a loud, clear, piercing cry of 'design!' The result is so unambiguous and so significant that it must be ranked as one of the greatest achievements in the history of science. The discovery rivals those of Newton, Einstein, Lavoisier and Schrödinger, Pasteur and Darwin.... The magnitude of the victory, gained at such great cost through sustained effort over the course of decades, would be expected to send champagne corks flying in labs around the world. This triumph of science should evoke cries of "Eureka" from ten thousand throats, should occasion much hand-slapping and high-fiving, and perhaps even be an excuse to take a day off.... Why does the scientific community not greedily embrace its startling discovery? [iv]

Nevertheless the perpetual discussion over the nature of man and the universe is one that may never be completed, and for a reason very well understood by the wise men of old. For, as the venerable Chinese text Tao de Ching points out, the true nature of the universe is something that cannot be known by the mind, it is literally beyond our comprehension in every way. And so, in a passage remarkably reminiscent of the Hymn of the Rig Veda, we learn that:

There is a thing confusedly formed
Born before heaven and earth
Silent and void
It stands alone and does not change
Goes round and does not weary.
It is capable of being the Mother of the world.
I know not its name
So I style it 'the way'.
I give it the makeshift name of 'the great'.
Tao, XXV, 56

The idea, which time and again we see repeated throughout the ancient teachings, is that the universe is created out of the formless, the 'uncarved block' of the Tao, and so is both indefinable and unimaginable. The seers in their meditation and visions appear to have seen this supreme consciousness as simply a void, but one which divides into a multitude of names and forms, to create the illusion of a universe and we the individuals who inhabit it.

23

These names and forms come from Maya, the Mother of illusion. And so we exist in a consciousness rooted in illusion, careering around in nothing more than an eternal cosmic game. It is only when we achieve self realisation, and awake to the reality that everything is actually formed from a single consciousness, that we are able to transcend the trials and tribulations of life and become a truly spiritual being – a yogi. This awakening is achieved through the union – or yoga – of our own individual drop of the universal spirit, the jivatman, with the universal aspect, the Paramatman.

It is perhaps not surprising that so many different names have been attached to this formless and universal spirit. The problem is that we cannot grasp the concept of something without a duality, we need to have a context within which to frame an idea in our imagination. We can talk about infinite space and we are able to contrast this with a finite space of any dimension. Similarly we can contrast good with evil, hot with cold or any 'normal' phenomena which we perceive with our mind. But to define a limitless, formless, timeless and unimaginable God is way beyond even our wildest fantasies. The best we can do is create a welter of names and illustrations with which to approximate our understanding.

That is why we resort to the creation of subsets of the Supreme; a pantheon of Deities, Incarnations and Prophets which allow us to grasp the reality of the spiritual universe. By giving name and form to that which is formless and unimaginable, we are able to focus on our journey towards the spirit. And in this way we each find a form or forms that we can be comfortable with, and which give us a solid handle on which to hang our meditation and prayer. To some, Lord Krishna, to others Lord Jesus Christ, the Lord Buddha or Allah the Merciful.

Unfortunately man has a habit of distorting the use of these stepping stones to God for his own purposes, thereby creating division and misery out of the unity and beauty of one Creator. We do ourselves no favours by twisting the truth in this way, but still we follow these divisive 'religions', almost out of habit. How ironic that the word religion actually comes from the ancient Latin 'religare', meaning 'to bind together or connect'.

Nevertheless if we examine the authentic ancient teachings it is clear that a true spiritual journey is really a process of self creation, one where we form our own universe of wonder through deep meditation and inner knowledge. Those who aspire to become Yogis, therefore, strive to tap into this spiritual knowledge through their meditation and so elevate themselves enough to dissolve into the One.

The Upanishad texts of India, an important part of the ancient Vedic writings which form so much of the basis of yoga, teach us that the spiritual universe can only be 'known' through this union and not through mere learning. For how can one paint the beauty of music, or listen to a sensuous pattern of colour; both need to be experienced in their own context in order to be appreciated properly.

The English poet Keats summed it up, perhaps, when he wrote in February 1818:

'Now it appears to me that almost any Man may, like the spider, spin from his own innards his own airy Citadel – the points of leaves and twigs on which the spider begins her work are few, and she fills the air with a beautiful circuiting. Man should be content with as few points to tip with the fine web of his Soul, and weave a tapestry empyrean, full of symbols for his spiritual eye, of softness for his spiritual touch, of space for his wanderings, of distinctness for his luxury.'[v]

The task facing those wanting to become Yogis, therefore, is simple. To move beyond the mere imaginings of the mind and literally transform into a spiritual being, melting into a glorious union with the eternal and infinite. To many this is nothing less than a fantasy, but for those with determination it is a goal which can and has been achieved through the diligent application of authentic yoga practices.

In the past, the only possible way of achieving this ultimate of tasks was through the deep and ascetic meditation of yoga, by which the energies in the subtle spiritual system inside each individual could be marshalled and put to proper use. Today these ancient practices have been brought up to date and incorporated into the teachings of Sahaja Yoga, which, with its tangible feedback and practical techniques, proves conclusively that the glory of real yoga is within the reach of every single human being on earth.

- CHAPTER TWO -

When the five senses and the mind are still, and reason itself rests in silence, then begins the Path supreme. This calm steadiness of the senses is called Yoga. Then one should become watchful, because yoga comes and goes. Katha Upanishad

ANCIENT KNOWLEDGE

Yoga has been around for a long time. Just how long no-one knows for sure, but suffice to say that scholars now believe that the earliest formal practise of 'archaic' yoga probably dates from the ancient Harappan civilisations of the Indus Valley (in what is now Afghanistan/Pakistan) around 7000 years ago.

An earthenware seal depicting a form in a Shiva-like cross legged posture, dating from around the 3rd millennium BC and associated with the Mohenjo Daro era, is thought to be the earliest hard evidence of a yoga discipline in existence at the time, and there are those who believe that the Rig Vedas (Knowledge of Praise) may have been formulated and passed down by word of mouth several thousand, or even tens of thousands of years earlier than that.

However old, it seems likely that yoga developed out of man's deepening relationship with the earth as civilisation dawned, a respect and reverence that took into account the changing seasons and their effect on harvests and hunting expeditions. A careful examination of the astonishingly sophisticated civilisations of those days – with their ritualistic burials and communal baths – suggests that this was a time when man began to question the nature of his existence with an increasing resolve, and where better to start than with an introspective review through inner contemplation?

It is also likely that the earliest form of yoga involved gifted 'Seers' who began to introspect and thereby produce their inspired visions of the connection between man and the Cosmos, the inner and outer spiritual cause. Through this deep meditation they were able to build a picture of the subtle spiritual system inside all of us, and relate this to the pattern of life and death. The fact that there were almost certainly a number of diverse and geographically separate revelations which produced a similar result would have given credence to this view of the complete link between man and God.

These insights were at first passed down by word of mouth from Seer to Seer, usually in the form of poems or cryptic depictions of the state of transcendental experience, and over time these oral recitations also began to include deep insights into all aspects of life, ranging from astronomy to science and mathematics.

Through these meditations, too, came a collection of Gods and universes which gave form to the formless, to help those not gifted with the 'inner sight' understand a little more about the beauty and power of the spiritual aspect of humankind. In turn these Gods and universes were slowly promoted to a form of ritualistic worship, which helped man rationalize his apparently random relationship with nature and providence. Our ancient ancestors literally began to spiritually sing for their supper!

To this day the early Vedas and the later associated texts known as the Upanishads, as passed down from wise man to disciple over thousands of years, are still a masterpiece of profound knowledge, albeit wrapped in a subtle prose that has still not been fully and completely deciphered. The practices based upon these mystical texts were probably not labelled as yoga in the early days, but it is clear that eventually the concept of Yuj - the Sanksrit root word meaning union, from which the word yoga derives – developed over time to form today's definition. These meditations were considered to be no less than a joining together of man and God in one consciousness, transcending all duality and material illusion.

TYPES OF YOGA

Today we know yoga as many things. To some it is a form of exercise, to others a formalised way of life, embodying elaborate ritual and incantation. At the heart of every form of yoga, however, lies the one truth – the need to achieve a union with God, a complete self knowledge and a merging of consciousness in the one universal spirit.

Perhaps the greatest exposition of yoga in its purest form comes from the seminal Indian classical work, The Bhagavad Gita. This poem, enclosed in the epic Mahabharata, depicts man's internal struggle for self knowledge, and for an understanding of God and the nature of the spirit. Central to the piece is the conversation between God, represented by Lord Krishna, and the soul of man, depicted by Arjuna.

In this conversation, Arjuna's tortured soul seeks a path to find its true nature and asks for help. Krishna's reply is to outline three forms of yoga - Karma, Jnana and Bhakti - which may be used as a route for us to attain our Moksha or liberation from the cage of material being. His gentle and patient replies to the questions posed by Arjuna provide some of the most detailed instruction on how to achieve self-realisation that exist in the literature. In essence Arjuna - and by implication humankind – is offered the paths of Life, Light and Love.

A constant yearning to know the Inner Spirit, and a vision of Truth which gives liberation: this is true wisdom leading to vision. All against this is ignorance. Now I shall tell thee of the End of wisdom. When a man know this he goes beyond death. It is Brahman, beginingless, supreme: beyond what is not.
His hands and feet are everywhere, he has heads and mouths everywhere: he sees all, he hears all. He is in all, and he is.
The Light of consciousness comes to him through infinite powers of perception, and yet he is above all these powers. He is beyond all, and yet he supports all. He is beyond the world of matter, and yet he has joy in this world. **Bhagavad Gita. 13 (11-14)**

Karma Yoga: The Path of Righteous Action

Through the diligent execution of our spiritual duty we can aspire to and achieve our spiritual salvation. This does not simply mean the performance of ritual or religious dogma, but a genuine focus on meeting our spiritual responsibilities in a heartfelt way.

Karma Yoga means that we can evolve through conscientious attention to our duties - spiritual and otherwise - and through a growing realisation that ultimately we are not the doer, we are merely a channel for the infinite and eternal divine will. In this way we build up our detachment and begin to eschew reward for our actions, and instead humbly lay all the fruits of our actions at the feet of God. It is this dissolution of our ego that brings us to the light of self realisation, as our spirit begins to manifest throughout every aspect of our actions and thoughts.

In Sahaja Yoga, it is this sense of duty - a deeply felt and reverent awareness of the responsibility to help others (known to the Chinese of Confuscius' days as Ching) - that is a key reason why yogi volunteers give up their time to hold free Sahaja meditation classes in venues across the world. By doing this genuinely selfless act, Sahaja Yogis are able to give back some of the joy they have received and also benefit from the deepening of their spirituality which comes from this form of Karma Yoga.

In its purest form Karma Yoga lets us renounce the illusion of this existence through elaborate spiritual routines and cleansing processes. It is a yoga of technique, and as such embodies the beauty and symmetry of action done with full attention on God. This aspect of yoga forms the core of many of the modern versions of the practise, including Hatha, Raja and Mantra Yoga.

Bhakti Yoga: The Path of Worshipful Devotion

When Arjuna complains about the difficulties in accomplishing yoga, Shri Krishna suggests an easier alternative - Bhakti, the love and worship of God in all forms. This yoga is based on the powerful love for God that flows from a recognition of the true nature of

Divinity. When this love becomes an intrinsic part of our lives and being, it transforms us into a collective soul devoted to the service of our fellows through worship of a unifying God. Through this dedicated focus and heartfelt action, the individual evolves to a state of self realisation and union with the adored One who exists as the divine spark, the life-force within all living beings and who permeates all the created universe.

This adoration comes from the heart and not from the mind, and so serves also to transform our experience of life from an ego oriented one, to one which exists purely on the spiritual plane. For God is Love and if we are awash in the essence of love we cannot fail to achieve our yoga, in a spontaneous and natural way, without effort or trial. It is Bhakti Yoga that lets us make full use of the relationship between ourselves and the Deities – Divinely invested spiritual beings and incarnations - who give a name and form to the spiritual universe. By focusing our love and gratitude on our Guru, teacher, favourite incarnation or prophet, we place our ego at their feet, and so move closer to our eventual release from Samsara, the cycle of birth and death.

The word worship has today become tainted by the excesses of modern religions. To worship someone or something is seen as a complete subjugation of our individual freedom, a sort of slavery of the mind. For this reason, anyone who talks of worshipping the Divine form is considered to be weak or deluded. But in its purest form worship is the ultimate freedom. We cannot worship in isolation, nor does it happen in some mechanical way, we cannot suddenly turn on a worship tap and bow down on demand.

The process begins with a gentle appreciation of the nature of God and the process of real religion. We come to recognize the signs of a truly benevolent relationship with our universe and its creator. After a time we may become truly grateful for the benefits – both internal and external - which come from our deepening relationship with this invisible benefactor. Which in turn begins to transform into a genuine love as we begin to realize that this is probably the first really truly purely unselfish relationship that we have ever experienced, that God gives without needing any response or return.

This is not just a case of material benevolence, and in fact that can be the least impressive aspect of this burgeoning relationship. The real proof of our growing spirituality is the inner peace that comes with it. Our bhakti, our worship, grows not through frivolous attention on material comfort, but from the gentle, loving response we feel building inside of us as we find our emotional and mental needs being fulfilled time after time, without pause. Even when we think that things are not going well, we will discover the truth and be astonished.

And so the yogi grows to love this relationship, this invisible bond, with all of the passion of their heart. Genuinely, without motive, without ego or temperament. The yogi sees all the love of God in every part of the creation, sees how it has been made especially to give pleasure to the inhabitants of the world. And this love becomes so over-powering, so all consuming that eventually it spontaneously transforms into worship, in the same way that a tiny baby worships its mother for constantly giving comfort, love, food and patience.

This is the real Bhakti Yoga, and the Bhaktas, those who practice and achieve their self-realization through this route, achieve their Moksha or liberation, with joy and single-minded devotion to the object of their worship.

Jnana Yoga: The Path of Light

This is a spiritual journey based around deep and profound knowledge through meditation. This yoga occurs as we move beyond the imperfections and delusions of the mind, and enter into the light of a truly spiritual awareness. Where Karma Yoga requires us to perform divinely sponsored actions, Jnana is a practise of complete inaction, of surrender to the gentle power of our sacred

Kundalini energy, which enlightens us by uniting our individual spirit with the infinite Cosmic Spirit.

This union floods our being with the knowledge of truth beyond the mind and intellect. We become the essence of spiritual thought, and through this absolute knowledge we become completely detached from desires, and thereby exist in a constant state of peace and joy. In Sahaja Yoga we experience this knowledge as a synthesis of all thought, wisdom and experience. We recognise the truth, and act on it, and because of it we are able to keep our attention focussed on the spiritual dimension continually.

The light of the knowledge of God transforms us and moves us on to the spiritual plane, to that magical fourth (turiya) state of being which is completely Divine. Such Jnana or knowledge cannot be known by the mind, which is why we need to experience the flowering of the Kundalini - the flow of energy from the base of the spine to the top of the head - in order to rise above the mind and become the knowledge. By becoming the light itself we are able to fuse with God and enter into a state of pure self awareness.

Jnana Yoga is the becoming. We do not practice yoga anymore, we become it instead, in the same way that the sun and sunlight are identical and yet separate entities. By becoming the knowledge, we also become the truth and thereby dissolve into the universal consciousness that is reality.

The yogi who has become the spiritual knowledge has no need to explain anything to anyone. They do not merely meditate, they are meditation incarnate. They have no questions, not because they have all the answers, but because there are no questions which they need to ask. They are complete beings.

THE MODERN WAY

This beautiful exposition of the pathways to God enunciated in the Gita, give us a truly profound insight into the direction that any genuine seeker of truth should take in order to achieve complete self awareness. It is based on a natural respect for the sanctity of God and points to an ancient way of life where an everyday communion between God and man was taken for granted. The individual's search for yoga in those days was no more than a natural extension of that relationship, and the eventual union was considered to be attainable by all right thinking people.

In many ways, the modern drift away from the core meaning of yoga is simply a reflection of the growing Western distaste for the distorted religious teachings that are peddled to us in the name of a rigid, hierarchical and twisted view of Divinity. This in turn has made us wary of trusting ourselves to anything that professes to lead towards increased godliness in general.

The result is a creeping Westernisation of yoga arranged in a series of easily assimilated formats - video friendly celebrities, exercise regimes, healing classes - all of which conveniently avoid any focus on God and thereby neatly sidestep potential conflicts with individual concepts of faith and religion. Concepts, which it has to be said, are often no more than a blindly conditioned acceptance of beliefs learned from childhood.

In many cases we tag ourselves as officially a follower of this or that religion simply because we grew up attending a church, temple, or other place of worship with our parents. In effect we end up adopting an uneasy relationship with faith, using it at moments of significance in our lives - births, deaths, weddings and disaster – merely, perhaps, to bolster our withering spiritual awareness.

We avoid mentioning our faith to friends and family in case we show weakness, or if we are 'born again' we go to the opposite extreme and try to push our faith onto others around us at every opportunity, as though to justify our blind allegiance to something, anything, that we can use as a crutch in an increasingly challenging world.

Perhaps we need to re-evaluate our real relationship with God and the spirit and determine what level of communication we really want and need?

SAHAJA YOGA AS A SYNTHESIS

Sahaja Yoga is a powerful fusion of all the ancient forms of yoga, and merges all the important features of these authentic routes to self knowledge. In the first instance Jnana Yoga is represented through the flowering of the sacred Kundalini energy. This spontaneous happening is the core component of the Sahaj process we undergo when we start meditating, and is the means by which Sahaja Yoga has brought mass self-realisation to the modern world. Without the simple and yet powerful cleansing action of the Kundalini, the journey towards true union would be very much more difficult, if not impossible.

Because the Kundalini is a conscious energy, She delivers gentle enlightenment through the power of cleansing. By nourishing our spiritual centres, She helps us to remember our true nature, to make us more detached, fearless, wise and loving. We become the spiritual witness through the gradual unfolding of our subtle spiritual flower. This is the true spiritual Jnana.

But the initial work of the Kundalini is only a single first step in bringing us closer to the spiritual universe. Our dedicated resolve to meditate provides the second vital ingredient, and it is here that Karma Yoga plays its part. The techniques of Sahaja Yoga that we use everyday support and enhance the work done by our Kundalini, so that the process of cleansing and spiritual elevation proceeds more efficiently. Accomplishing our yoga requires a diligent and hard working attitude, but one that must be done without ego.

We perform our daily meditations to show our genuine and pure desire to evolve into a spiritual being. And so we rise above our Karmas and above the mind by laying the fruits of our progress at the feet of God. The real test of any form of yoga is whether we are able to strive for our spiritual evolution without identifying with the ego of the process. We behave as though we are witnessing the act from a distance. In our Sahaj meditation we focus on becoming detached from our practice in just this way.

The final piece of the jigsaw involves the opening of our heart. When we begin to experience real joy in meditation, we also start to recognise the Divine source of all reality, and thereby develop a deep love and respect for the whole creation. This deepening understanding forms the core of our spiritual faith, and because it is such a rich and rewarding experience we naturally start to cherish our burgeoning relationship with the whole wonderful Divine universe.

The Bhakti or devotion, develops spontaneously as we grow in our spirituality, in many ways marking off the distance along our route to salvation. We not only grow to love our world and fellow travellers on the road, but also, crucially, to experience genuine devotion to God in all forms – and from the heart, not just the mind. All of the different aspects of the same one God - our Guru or teacher, Mother Nature in all Her glory, the spirit within each of us - become objects of a genuine, deep seated and passionate veneration. And in some beautiful and Divine dance we receive, in return, wave upon wave of unequivocal, unquestioning love, flowing through us and through our lives like the purest rivers of heaven.

It is probably fair to say that there is no form of yoga which combines these key ingredients in such a powerful, effective and tangible way as Sahaja Yoga. Other practices may offer various combinations of these spiritual features, but the Sahaj method is the only one to incorporate all of the key parts of ancient yoga in one complete package. Its focus on union - the process of awakening the Kundalini to achieve self realisation – and adherence to all of the authentic forms of ancient yoga make it a unique form of spiritual activity. Practitioners quickly learn to apply their growing spiritual qualities to their everyday lives, and experience the kind of joy and peace which can only come from a genuine spiritual transformation.

The rich spiritual tapestry of this yoga also ensures that each individual can journey at their own pace and in a way that suits their own temperament and characteristics.

INTRODUCTION TO SAHAJA YOGA

You are not this body, this mind, these conditionings, this ego. You are nothing but the true Spirit. Shri Mataji Nirmala Devi.

The term Sahaja Yoga derives from the Sanskrit meaning of the words. Saha means 'spontaneous' or 'born with', ja means 'you' and yoga translates as 'union'. Sahaja Yoga then translates as *'the spontaneous method of Divine union that everyone is born with'*. This union is achieved through a process called self-realisation, which is the flowering of a conscious but dormant energy inside each of us known as the Kundalini.

What is Self Realisation?

In the sacrum bone at the base of the spine in every individual there is a subtle and dormant coil of spiritual energy known as the Kundalini. This energy has been well documented down through the ages, and is a core part of all genuine yoga and spiritual practice. In AD1290, for instance, the renowned Indian saint and mystic Jnanadeva documented in detail the existence of this energy in his seminal treatise on yoga and the spiritual universe, the Jnaneshwari.

The Goddess Kundalini is verily like the very Mother of the Universe, as also the grandeur of the Supreme Majesty of soul . . . She looks as if she is cast in the image of the life-breath clad in a yellow coloured cloth of gold, but just discarding it and getting exposed, or as a lamp-flame getting extinguished by a breeze of wind, or as a lightning just flashing in the sky and then just disappearing. **Jnaneshwari, Chap. 6, Vs 14.**

The process of self-realisation involves the gentle awakening of this living and conscious energy, so that it pervades the individual's entire subtle (i.e. spiritual) being. The flowering of the Kundalini has to be accomplished under the right circumstances, which historically used to involve extensive and arduous spiritual practises

37

often over the course of many lifetimes. Today Sahaja Yoga provides the experience in a split of a second.

Once the Kundalini is awakened in this way, she nourishes and cleanses the whole of the individual's subtle system - including the Chakras (energy centres) and Nadis (energy channels) - thereby ensuring that they can achieve a state of balance in their lives and so make the all important journey towards becoming a spiritually enlightened person.

After the initial moment of self-realisation has occurred and the Kundalini is awakened to her full potential, the person is no longer isolated from the universe around them – i.e. trapped inside their own head – but becomes a connected part of the greater cosmos.

The benefits of this awakening are many, including a realisation of our sense of purpose, a feeling of completeness and the sort of self-knowledge which is commonly missing from our day to day lives and activities.

From that point on, it is up to the individual to decide whether they wish to explore the new world that opens up to them, by continuing with a programme of meditation to enhance and encourage the gentle power of this marvellous living energy.

Introduction to the meditation

The meditation is a deceptively simple process and takes the form of sitting quietly to allow the Kundalini to rise from its seat at the base of the spine to the top of the head - along the central spiritual 'channel' inside all of us, the Sushumna Nadi. Again many literary works dealing with yoga describe this subtle road map; this is knowledge which has been available for thousands of years, not merely a few centuries.

This Kundalini energy cleanses the individual's Chakras – or spiritual centres – and by gently subduing the mental activity of the ego and super ego during the course of her journey, leaves the person in a profoundly peaceful and relaxed state. Practitioners also use a variety of techniques – including simple mantras and gestures – to help improve the depth and quality of their meditation, and to attain a state known as 'thoughtless awareness' or 'nirvichara samadhi'.

As practitioners become more adept in the process, they learn how to actively monitor the state of their own subtle system, in order to move themselves back into balance when necessary. They learn also how to decipher the subtle energy flows of other people, and so can work with them to help them achieve a deeper state of meditation.

Above all, the meditation gives one a growing level of self knowledge. This awareness can be used to improve every aspect of ones life, from the simplest need to the most profound.

– CHAPTER THREE –

As far as we can discern, the sole purpose of human existence is to kindle a light in the darkness of mere being. Carl Jung (1875–1961)

KNOW THYSELF – THE SUBTLE SYSTEM

We are an incredibly intricate spiritual mechanism, wrapped up in the flesh and bone of this physical universe. Nevertheless, the exhortation to *'know thyself'* is often taken to require nothing more than a sort of intellectual examination of our personality. But in reality, real self-knowledge comes not from the mind, but from an experiencing of – and eventually a fusion with – our own complex spiritual system.

The ancient Seers literally spent their whole lives in deepest meditation, trying to unravel the form and function of this most mysterious and subtle system. Many introspections ended up frustratingly fruitless and empty, but from the few who managed to achieve genuine enlightenment, we have gained an invaluable understanding of the subtle spiritual instrument, energy channels and Chakras.

Many of these insights must also have been accompanied by direct physical sensations, which were then used to track these subtle energy flows and prove their existence outside of the meditative state.

No one can say exactly when the subtle map of the spiritual body was first drawn up, but it almost certainly mirrored man's search for more than just physical comfort and food, which indicates that it could have been developed over 10,000 years ago.

Through the amazing and consistent work done by these ancient sages, we now have a structured picture of the subtle body as containing a multitude of invisible spiritual channels and centres, called Nadis and Chakras respectively, through which flow our vital spiritual energies. The Nadis act as roadways for our spiritual energy, moving it around the system in an effort to maintain balance and nourishment for the whole being.

The Chakras are junctions of this energy, and also represent meeting points between the physical and spiritual bodies. The Chakras are important because of their relationship with our senses and their interaction with our mind and consciousness. In many ways the Chakras work as filters and regulators of our perception and interaction with the physical reality.

This incorporeal, and yet so important, subtle body therefore clearly provides the basic framework of our existence. It is the ultimate home of our consciousness and soul, and the network which sustains the 'spark' of life by which we exist in this material illusion of time and space. Unless we take the time to understand how it is built and its importance in relation to our overall being, we will have trouble using its power to help drive our spiritual transformation.

The energy flows contained in this system also affect two subtle areas of the brain which contribute to our character and personality – the ego and super ego. The ego, which is situated on the left side of the brain area (see Fig 1 below), controls our thinking, planning and action. It is linked with the right spiritual channel, and is a vital part of our day to day actions – in effect we DO because of it.

The super ego resides on the right hand side of the brain area and is linked to the left subtle channel. It houses our deepest emotional characteristics and our conditionings, built up from a lifetime of thoughts and experiences. It is directly responsible for how we 'feel' about something – we ARE what we are because of it.

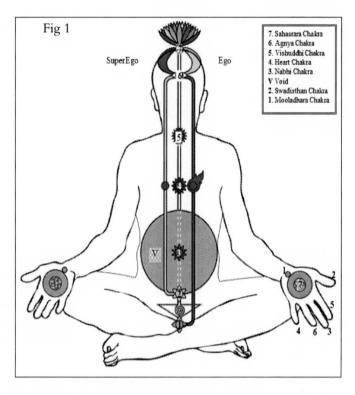

Fig 1

SuperEgo   Ego

7. Sahasrara Chakra
6. Agnya Chakra
5. Vishuddhi Chakra
4. Heart Chakra
3. Nabhi Chakra
V Void
2. Swadisthan Chakra
1. Mooladhara Chakra

We should not pretend to understand the world only by the intellect; we apprehend it just as much by feeling. Therefore the judgment of the intellect is, at best, only the half of truth, and must, if it be honest, also come to an understanding of its inadequacy.[vi] Carl Jung.

In normal day to day activity, a complex interaction between left and right channel, ego, super ego and the Chakras, all combine to produce our own personal universe and interaction with it. We exhibit particular emotional responses to some sensory stimuli, and commit certain acts in response to others. We may, for instance, become angry with someone who has emotionally hurt us, and take action to erase them from our life by ripping up their photograph or throwing out their clothes. These are interactions which involve the whole of our subtle and emotional mechanism, acting in concert.

The energies ebb and flow, wax and wane according to internal and external stimuli or events, although in fact this movement can be thought of more properly as a change of state rather than an alteration in volume or intensity. When we talk of the movement of spiritual energy throughout a subtle body, we actually mean subtle shifts in composition – beyond our understanding, but nonetheless just as real. These changes occur both collectively and individually, and if we remember that we all exist as part of a great ocean of energy, we can see just how delicately interwoven this whole spiritual tapestry is.

THE EGO AND SUPER EGO

Our ego is the means by which we make our way through life, without it we would simply sit and vegetate. Our sense of 'I', our mental awareness of self and our drive to accomplish necessary tasks are all driven by the ego, and it is a perfectly natural part of our human makeup. However, problems can arise when we become too identified with this sense of I-ness. When this happens we become increasingly isolated from the world and begin to lose sight of our true relationship with the cosmic ocean in which we exist.

The super ego is that part of us which relates to our emotional makeup, in effect the home of our conditionings. As we mature, this subtle entity interacts with our ego to reinforce our personal viewpoint of the world, creating and refining our prejudices and opinions. Without the work done by the super ego we would not be able to take full advantage of the marvels of our memory, and so would have trouble making our way through the convoluted pathways of life. This combination of experience and emotion provides much of the rich fabric of our personality. However if we become excessively governed by this side of our person, we can become unstable and maybe even prone to bouts of irrational behaviour.

The interaction between the ego, super ego and the energy channels of the subtle body is an intricate and important part of our day to day existence. We make sense of our surroundings, take actions and respond to external events and stimuli through the use of our senses and our mind, which in turn are governed by the flow of energy through our subtle system.

When we are in a state of mental and emotional equilibrium and living a balanced life, we take advantage of the proper energy flows and maintain a stable existence. However it is almost impossible for most of us who live a hectic modern lifestyle to maintain this balanced state for any length of time. Sooner or later we are beset by problems or events which send us careering off centre. It is at these times that we can find that our ego and super ego lead us into further distress by reacting and over-reacting to situations.

If, for instance, we become over stressed through our work or pressures at home, we affect the flow of energy on the right channel, which, as we will see later, means that the channel becomes overheated. This in turn affects the ego which in symbolic terms inflates and becomes more active as a result of the heat. This can then lead us into taking unwise action, flying into unreasonable and surprising rages, or even in the more severe cases into mental breakdown.

We all know people who are egotistical, and this often just means that they have been over using their right channel for so long without respite, that their ego has become permanently bloated, to the extent that they start to believe that they are superior to others around them. Egoism is no more than a disease of the right side, and can be treated as such, if only the person has enough of an incentive to want to change.

Unfortunately such people rarely do wish to change, especially if they hold positions of power, wealth or responsibility, unless they receive a life threatening shock which makes them take stock of their lives and humble down.

On the left side, the super ego works to make us more creative, and balances out the action orientation of our right side by housing our emotional sensibilities. When it is in a balanced state, our super ego can drive us to produce astounding works of art, and can power astonishing levels of heartfelt compassion and deep feelings in our personality. The super ego is the wellspring of our insight, pure inspiration and spiritual sensitivity.

However, if we allow our emotional makeup and prejudices to dominate our personality they can make us blind to the truth. We can become so wrapped up in our beliefs and our view of life that we close our minds and hearts to the truth that others can see clearly. Ironically the bloated ego often gives fuel to the bloated super ego, as one tries furiously to counter balance the unbalancing effects of the other. That's why we often see that people in power become outrageously prejudiced and perhaps even bigoted as their ego and super ego bloat and collide in a battle for domination within the subtle system. Similarly, a chronic tendency to an excess of super ego alone can lead to a lack of alertness and dynamism, and a drift towards lethargy and even depression.

Through meditation we can soothe down these two entities and bring about stability in the energy flows which feed them. In this way the potentially damaging effects of the oscillation between bloated ego and super ego can be avoided completely. In a balanced and spiritually oriented personality, the two work together and project their most positive qualities to ensure that the actions and thoughts of that soul reflect more accurately the Divine will and true human spirit. It is impossible for the ego or super ego to dominate such a person for any length of time, because each meditation restores the balance of energies in the whole subtle body, and so soothes them down to a more stable state of equilibrium.

The ego and super ego are a vital part of our being, and are designed to work in a harmonious relationship with the whole of the subtle system. However when we are exposed to a difficult or harmful environment, or we start to lose our balance for other reasons, then these components begin to function discordantly. Eventually, if this discord continues for long enough, our spiritual energy flows start to change state in an uncontrolled, unpredictable and increasingly random way.

KUNDALINI

The Kundalini is the instrument of spiritual evolution. This feminine energy is situated at the base of the spine, occupying a space inside the area of the Sacrum bone. She is a conscious energy, in that she is aware and responds to appropriate stimuli, and She is resident in every human being from birth, but in a dormant state.

When she becomes aware of our devoted and conscientious desire to become a true yogi, she awakens and by so doing, energises the whole of the subtle, spiritual system inside our body. She then undertakes a journey to the top of the head during which She cleanses the Chakras and nourishes the parts of our system that need it.

Without the Kundalini there can be no yoga, for our loving Kundalini is the Divine instrument within us all that makes our yoga happen. Although sparsely documented, Kundalini has been associated with yoga and authentic spirituality for thousands of years, and mentioned in some of the most important spiritual books and writings. In Jnanadeva's exposition of the Bhagavad Gita, the Jnaneshwari, he describes in detail just how powerful the Kundalini is when She flowers as part of an adept's yoga meditation.

'Kundalini is one of the greatest energies. The whole body of the seeker starts glowing because of the rising of the Kundalini. Because of that, unwanted impurities in the body disappear. The body of the seeker suddenly looks very proportionate and the eyes look bright and attractive and the eyeballs glow.' **Jyaneshwari, Chapter VI**

Kundalini is the feminine aspect of God made manifest. It is only because of Her loving, compassionate and tireless work cleansing the Chakras in our subtle system, that we grow in spirituality

46

through meditation. She it is who crosses the 'ocean of illusion' thereby giving us our self-realisation and without Her work in piercing through the Sahasrara Chakra we would never be able to transcend the mind and attain true yoga.

Mother Kundalini helps remove the restrictive aspects of our ego and super ego, and so gives us vital space to achieve the state of 'thoughtless awareness' that is the key to Sahaja Yoga meditation. Without this we would never be able to slow the pace of our thoughts, and would therefore be anchored forever at the material, conscious level of the mind.

She cools down the heat in our right channel when it becomes over excited, and warms up our left channel when it becomes too cold, and so ensures that we maintain a constant state of spiritual balance.

Most importantly of all, She is the one who responds to our desire, our subtle desire, to grow in spirituality. Every time we take our place for meditation, She responds to our pure desire and immediately starts Her work cleansing, clearing, soothing and calming our spiritual channels and Chakras. Only through Her work can an adept ever achieve real yoga.

Everything else is simply false.

THE THREE CHANNELS
The invisible Subtle Body contains a number of channels along which run vital spiritual energies, which in turn make up the essence of our spiritual being. The exact number of these Nadis (meaning channel) is unknown, although some writings have suggested that there could be more than 70,000.

Other practises believe that there are 14 primary channels, but in Sahaja Yoga teachings only three of these are considered to be really crucial. These are the Ida, Pingala and Sushumna Nadis – or the Left, Right and Central Channels respectively.

Ida Nadi.

This is the moon channel, the Yin. This is the part of us which is associated with our emotional and feminine qualities and which relates to our past actions. This channel nourishes us with all that is beautiful in terms of our soft artistic qualities and the gentleness of true humanity. It is also the power behind our true desires. When we are living in a balanced state we draw upon the energy of this channel to produce art, offer worship and display spiritual depth in our actions.

The Ida Nadi is very much the passive side of our being, and as such gives us the power to love and witness. We also utilise the power of the Ida Nadi when we learn from the mistakes of the past, and exhibit respect for the wisdom and teachings of the ancients. This is also the channel of the mother, and so embodies all of the important aspects of love and compassion that are such a powerful part of the human condition. Without the compassion of the mother, we would not be the people we are.

This channel is represented by the colour blue which indicates the moon and coolness. When we overuse or abuse this channel it becomes too cold and so we slip into an increasingly lethargic, or even depressed, state. The best way to compensate for any such overuse, therefore, is to try to warm up the channel with light and heat.

Pingala Nadi.

The Sun channel, the Yang and the side of us which is associated with the masculine, with action and with the dynamism of our future actions. This channel is the energy source which powers our doing. From this side we translate the desire to be creative which comes from the Ida Nadi, into the creation of the actual artistic piece. Without the right channel we would not be able to function as normal human beings, and do the things we need to do to survive and flourish. We derive our optimism from this channel, and the capacity to overcome any adversity in our search for truth. When we are living a balanced life this channel provides the fuel we need to help flower our compassion and so assist others in a generous and heartfelt way.

The channel is represented by the colour yellow, which indicates sun and heat. The channel embodies the principle of the father, and as such it helps us exhibit the benevolent discipline which is needed if we are to live together in an orderly way in our relationships and in society at large. When we overuse this channel it becomes too hot and we become over heated in our actions and behaviour. In order to return to balance we need to cool it down with ice, cooling foods and soothing environments like the beauty of nature.

Sushumna Nadi.

The central channel is the channel of light. It is the path to our ultimate evolution, the channel along which our Kundalini travels on Her way to effecting our ultimate yoga. Whereas the Ida Nadi is a reflection of our past and the Pingala our future, the Sushumna is the present, the here and now. When we are in balance, we use the Sushumna channel to draw on the silence and the power of every passing moment. In effect we live for the present and by so doing we experience all the wonderful things that the 'now' has to offer.

These three Nadis are reflections of the primordial Gunas - Rajas, Tamas and Satva - the three states of being within which all things exist. In the traditional Indian Vedantic philosophy these states, or qualities, are part of the illusion (or Maya) of existence – in other words they constitute the building blocks of all that we know or think is real. Rajas corresponds to the right channel, to the flow of activity that is associated with the creation. Tamas is the power of veiling, which hides the true nature of reality, which in turn equates to the left channel reflected in man's sloth and uncertainty.

Satva is the primordial aspect of evolution reflected in the central channel, and balances the two other Gunas. It is a state of purity and unselfishness which leads to the truth of existence. The evolutionary power of the Satvic state keeps any negative influences of the Rajas and Tamas states in check. When we finally evolve spiritually to the ultimate state of being, we move beyond the influence of the three Gunas in the same way that we transcend the effect of the energy flows through our Nadis. Our yoga literally takes us beyond the three states and into a fourth (or Turiya) state which is purely spiritual.

EFFECT OF NADI ENERGY FLOWS ON OUR DAY TO DAY LIVES

As we go through life our spiritual energies are in a perpetual and natural state of flux. Some channels become exhausted while others are enriched, and we are subject to a constant interaction between our internal spiritual flows and those of our environment and in other people. For this reason it is important to recognise our subtle strengths and weaknesses in order that we can maintain a state of balance more effectively throughout each day.

The flow of energy through our subtle energy channels has a direct impact on our lives in every way. If there is too much energy from the right channel – our action side – flowing into the ego, we can quickly become very egotistical and out of touch with reality and the truth. If too much energy from the left channel – our emotional side - flows into the superego, we can become lethargic or even depressed. Remember that when we talk about energy flows, we really mean changes in state, a sort of pulsing of energy through the system, rather than a flowing river type of action.

The flow of energy into and through our Chakras also affects our emotional and physical states. Even though we may think that the world exists independently of our state of being, the ancients recognized that how we 'are' at any one time has a direct affect on almost all of our existence. Contrast the state of someone who is 'in love' – carefree, happy, forgiving – with someone who is bereaved. Look at those who are always ill or grumpy and contrast them with those who are optimistic about life. And so on.

The way we approach life, and the way we handle different experiences is strongly affected by the different sensitivities in our

50

subtle system. Some of us, for example, are born more 'right sided', that is we use more of the action oriented energies of our right channel. In simple terms we are the 'constantly busy' type of person. Others, however, are born 'left sided', and use more of their emotional left channel. These people may be more laid back, sensitive souls, prone to bouts of introspection and self criticism. These innate tendencies are also affected by the constant buffeting we receive every day from our environment and other people's projected energies, so it's easy to see how and why we often end up living a roller-coaster kind of life which appears to be totally out of control.

The subtle system therefore is a mechanism which has a direct bearing on how we approach life, live life and cope with events in our lives. As such it is very important to keep our energy flows as stable as possible by keeping the Chakras clear and ourselves in a state of 'balance', whereby we do not over use the energies from either side.

What do we mean by over use?
Let's look at a couple of examples from both channels. It's been a tough day at work. You're behind on a project, your boss is hassling you by the hour to complete a task. You've got ten important things to do before you head off on holiday in 4 days time, and your sister is expecting you over for a meal tonight, even though you can't really spare the time.

This is a classic case where you could be over using the energy of the right channel. Irritation and stress, planning for future things like holidays, trying to juggle hectic social arrangements. It's unsettling. In Sahaj terms, unbalanced.

The other side. Your father is quite ill, and you have just lost your job as part of a company wide redundancy programme. The weather in this part of winter is nasty, dark and rainy. You have had a bitter row with your partner because you feel under pressure all round, and you think you're coming down with some sort of cold or flu. In these circumstances it's easy to get depressed, to sink into a sort of lonely, insecure mood which can't be lifted no matter how hard you try.

In this case we're over using the energy of the left channel, the moon side, our emotional side. We can feel the lethargy, and the unsettling effect this has on our overall mood. Again we're in an unbalanced state.

We all live through these kinds of states to one extent or another, and for the most part we cope as well as we can. But even the with the best will in the world, most of us come to a stage at some point where it all becomes just too much. It gets on top of us. It is at this point, when we really can't cope, that we're most vulnerable to illness or trauma, either stress generated or depression oriented. We may even require medication.

Every time we are exposed to an situation which is unbalanced, be it a stress filled office, a depressing funeral or any combination of unwelcome news, we take on a measurable amount of the negative energy that the situation generates. This in turn can knock us more off balance, aggravate our own negative tendencies and over time add to our overall vulnerability on all levels. We may not even notice this creeping fragility until one day something snaps and we end up completely incapacitated.

Every day we move through life coping with events which pummel the state of our spiritual energies. For example in the morning we may wake up bright and breezy and suddenly receive a letter containing a demand for an unexpectedly large amount of money we owe. This shock to the system can immediately throw us into a new state of being. From being happy, we may move to being angry or even depressed.

These states are not simply emotionally driven, but have at their root a change in the flow of energy through the three channels. For instance, anger heats up our right side. This in turn can increase our rage as we start thinking about the injustice of the demand or whatever. Conversely, depression or fatigue is a symptom of an over-cooling of the left channel. We may suddenly feel lonely and unable to cope with things, sliding into an uncharacteristic slump.

All of these examples are things that we commonly experience and generally we believe that they're caused by nothing more than emotional or physical reasons. 'Oh you're just over tired', 'just getting over the shock', 'over reacting'. We use all of these phrases to indicate that we're simply victims of various externally triggered emotional and environmental forces. But in fact we are not as victimised as we may think, we are simply reacting on a deeply subtle level to the spiritual forces acting on our lives.

In general most of us are too desensitised to feel these effects on our spiritual system, but when we achieve the awakening of self-realisation and our Kundalini starts flowing properly, we regain our lost sensitivity almost immediately, and start to use our subtle body to keep ourselves in a balanced state. Once we become 'realised souls', we learn how important our spiritual side is and learn how to cope with life's ups and downs and still keep ourselves in a balanced and stable state.

The energies which flow through our subtle spiritual system interact with our physical body via the central, sympathetic and parasympathetic nervous systems - which regulate the 'automatic' physical aspects of the human body, such as heart rate, digestion, blood vessel constriction etc - and as they do so they change states.

In subtle terms, we can say that the energy of any particular channel can change into an 'exhausted' state if it is 'over-used', or is in a 'balanced state' if it is flowing properly. So for instance the energy of the right channel can become 'overheated' through over use, or the left channel can become 'overcool'. Both of these changes of state - which are absolutely subtle and not caused by physical alterations in the body - have an effect on the ego or super ego to which the channel is connected, which in turn can have a knock on effect on the whole subtle body and its state of balance.

As we've seen, a mild oscillation between the energy flows in this way is perfectly natural. For example we often over-use the energies of the right side when we need to accomplish something important in a hurry, and conversely the left when we need to draw urgently on our motivational or creative strengths.

This is a conventional process which happens to all of us every day. However the stresses and strains of modern living have nowadays created an environment where we are expected to continually over exert ourselves in an unnatural manner, simply to keep pace with the demands of work, relationships and urban living.

This can completely disrupt the natural movement of energy flows around the subtle body in a dangerously uncontrolled way. Left unchecked, this oscillation can become wild and extreme, and so adversely impact our physical, mental and spiritual being. Constantly see-sawing between one extreme energy state and another – in effect swinging between extreme action and extreme lethargy - will eventually produce severely unpleasant effects in our lives. Those who rush around too much and overuse the energy of the right channel can become hugely stressed and suffer all the associated physical problems that such tension brings, whilst those who overuse the left channel can slide dangerously into depression and worse.

What makes these volatile swings even more hazardous is the fact that the natural state of human existence is equilibrium. Our spiritual system automatically and continually tries to compensate for any unnatural oscillations in energy, maintain equilibrium between the left and right channels, and thereby encourage us to use the energy of the central channel more. The central channel is the channel of our evolution, which is the fundamental destiny of every human being. Unless we evolve, we decay.

So when our system starts to go out of balance, every part of our being automatically attempts to re-establish some sort of stability, which in turn produces its own uncomfortable oscillation. We may for instance become very depressed, and to combat it instinctively try to 'keep busy'. This in turn may make us feel over tired, and lead to physical exhaustion, which drives us even further into the doldrums of the left side. And so on.

OUR SUBTLE CHARACTERISTICS

We've already seen that each of us tends to have a particular subtle personality trait which corresponds with the makeup of our subtle system. For instance we may notice that there are people who have been born with a tendency to over use their left channel energies, are more emotional, slower to action and may exhibit more of a creative streak. Those whose personalities are naturally more right sided, have a tendency to over use the energy of the right channel, and will be more dynamic, easily prone to stress and stress related illness and be more mental in their approach to life.

Similarly in its more extreme form, the over heating of a right sided person's system may incline them to become more egotistical as their ego inflates with the added strain of this altered energy state. It is almost as if the ego blows up with the hot exhaust fumes from the weakened and overworked right channel. On the left side, the extreme result of our imbalance may be a person who becomes sly and devious, or someone who will avoid responsibility at all costs.

Once we know exactly what to look out for, we can start to make allowances for the differences in others, and in our own case start to take steps to improve the balance of our spiritual energies through our meditation.

Symptoms of a left sided personal tendency

The left channel – or Ida Nadi – is our moon side, and as such it is associated with our feelings of lethargy, introversion and even depression. It is also the centre related to our desire, including the desire to acquire, achieve and even to live. Some of the most

55

creative souls in history have been strongly left side oriented, as it is the channel most associated with the creative arts of all types.

Left sided people will often be quite lethargic and inactive. They may be attracted to sadness or over emotional entertainment or even subject to sudden bouts of depression for no obvious reason. They may be unable or unwilling to take responsibility for anything, and try to avoid commitment. They can be quite introverted in many ways.

Many left sided personalities do, however, subconsciously try to compensate for the tendency by deliberately driving themselves to hard work and futuristic occupations. This type of workaholic can often be identified by their reluctance to take any sort of rest or vacation no matter how tired they are, lest they fall back into their natural left sided ways.

Left sided people tend to take a negative view of everything. Any situation, even the most trivial, which goes against their personal goals can wound them deeply. Eventually they can slump into a deep depression over the slightest thing, convinced that they are a victim of life. They may also suffer through relationships, convinced that they are the victim of a lack of understanding. In general the slightest action has the potential to leave a deep scar, and wound their fragile persona.

As well as these general personality traits, which come from our particular sensitivity to an energy channel, we are also subject to temporary shifts in our state of being, caused by external and internal changes in our energy levels and states.

So for example the following signs may indicate that we are over exhausting the energy of the left channel:
Feelings of loneliness.
Exhaustion and lethargy
Excessive focus on past events.
Depression and over emotional feelings

Symptoms of a right sided personal tendency

The right channel – or Pingala Nadi – is our hot side, and as such it is associated with our tendencies towards action, the future and planning. It is also the channel which is related to our feelings of responsibility, which can drive us to assume responsibility for something even if it has nothing to do with us directly.

Right sided people are very action oriented. They are always on the go, planning for this, organising that. Never a moment's peace or rest, happy only when doing. They are fond of action in all its forms and can never sit still. A moment wasted is a moment lost forever. They often try and take on the troubles of the world, even to the detriment to their own life or health. They can also quickly lose their sense of perspective when faced with a crisis or - more to the point - what they believe to be a crisis.

A right sided personality will never take no for an answer, nor allow themselves to show any form of weakness. The result is that they live a life full of stress, often in danger of collapsing under the weight of an unsustainable work load. They are the dominant, maybe even insensitive partner in their relationships. For them the world has to keep up, fit in with their timetable, even if sometimes that means they have to ride roughshod over other people's needs and desires.

We can recognise if we are slipping into a temporary right sided state by the following signs:

Unusual irritability, aggressiveness or anger
General over activity
Excessive planning and future watching/worrying
Domineering attitude
Insensitivity to others

The wonder of Sahaja Yoga is that for the first time ever, we are given the tools which can literally change our lives and our personality traits. We are no longer doomed to remain locked in a depressive or manic personality, nor do we have to remain victims of our environment. Through our meditation we can wash away the affects of an adverse environment and, over time, gently reset our innermost character flaws to give ourselves a more stable and balanced outlook on life. We can literally take the reins of our existence and steer a new and improved course for ourselves as we wish.

THE CHAKRA SYSTEM

There are seven major Chakras – or spiritual centres - in the Subtle Body (see also Appendix A for a more detailed explanation of the centres). These Chakras can be thought of as junction points, where energy flows intersect and are directed throughout the subtle body. The word Chakra means 'wheel' in Sanskrit, which comes from the fact that these centres are shaped like wheels, constantly rotating in synch to the Divine rhythm of life.

Our Chakras also interact with our physical side, control the operation of our bodily functions and affect both our senses and consciousness through links with our nervous and hormonal systems. In fact they play a vital part in every single aspect of our existence, and also have a crucial role in determining how we experience our world day to day. This is because our mind obtains its sensory input through the subtle filter of the Chakras, which means that they need to be in a cleansed, nourished and fully open state in order to ensure that our mind and body are in natural and perfect equilibrium.

Even the individual cells of our body are connected in this way, and receive their vital subtle nourishment from the spiritual system. When we talk about the good health of a person in a holistic sense, we mean the complete system working in harmony, with physical and spiritual aspects combining to provide total well-being. Once this subtle communion is broken for whatever reason, whether it's because of stress brought on by excessive mental exertion or depression brought on by emotional frustration, we can become prone to ill health and physical problems.

This Chakra system also plays a huge part in our journey of spiritual self discovery. We learn much about the nature of reality and the universe through a process of self examination and through meditating on the specific aspects of each individual Chakra. Every 'wheel' reflects a fundamental human quality which makes us what we are. These qualities are primordial, eternal and a part of the being of everyone who lives. As such they cannot be destroyed, only obscured by the blindness caused by our material existence.

Much of the power of the Chakras comes from the fact that they are the subtle home of the spiritual archetypes which have taken birth down the ages to help us rediscover the truth of our spiritual heritage. These prophets and avatars have their spiritual seat in every one of the Chakras, and meditating on them helps enormously in the process of cleansing each Chakra. It is the powerful spiritual quality of these archetypes, their Divine Power if you will, that does this important task, by responding to our respectful and heartfelt desire. When we need help and spiritual sustenance, we only have to ask and they will respond instantly to come to our aid.

Unfortunately the Chakras can become constricted through neglect. In their unrealised state, before the touch of Kundalini has given them Divine purpose, they operate in a semi-dormant form. In this desensitised state they react dully to our environment, and may only become discernible at times of massive trauma. Their power to heal and nourish is therefore severely limited and they are outside the conscious control of the body in which they operate.

Once they have been lovingly brushed by the Kundalini energy on Her journey through the subtle body, the Chakras begin to open up completely and reach their full potential. Not only do they stimulate the flow of spiritual energy through our system, but they also begin to re-establish the fundamental human qualities in our personality as a by-product of our spiritual awakening. These primordial qualities are not mental or psychological, but are eternal aspects of the spiritual dimension, bestowed on our individual Souls by the universal Soul. Once they begin to manifest we can truly start to recognise our full potential in every way. This is the beginning of our glorious journey of self knowledge.

The cleansing of our Chakras significantly improves the flow of energy through our channels. In their pre-enlightened state, we can say that the Chakras act as passive doorways to our spiritual energy. Once the centres have become enlightened, they take on a much more dynamic and active role in enriching the state of our energy flows, and improve our lives in many amazing ways.

The flow of energy through the Chakras helps to restore our innate spiritual personality, and so rebuild the tapestry of our true character. Each of the Chakras also interacts powerfully with the others, which in turn helps to determine the texture and direction of our spiritual journey. We literally create our own voyage of self discovery through our meditation and the cleansing of the Chakras and the Nadis. This is one of the ways that we truly do become our own master and guru.

Although there are many different Chakras which govern specific duties in the system, the seven main ones are the most commonly documented. It is these seven which deliver most of our spiritual strength, and it is through them that our physical, mental and spiritual being is kept in a state of harmony. All of the Chakras – apart from the Sahasrara - have multiple aspects which reflect their relationship to the three main Nadis. So, for example, we can say that the Heart (or Anahata) Chakra has a left, right and centre aspect, each of which reflect different areas of our spiritual and human personality.

By focussing on each of the Chakras, and these different aspects, we can gradually build a strong and powerful subtle system which will carry us wherever we need to go in our spiritual odyssey.

Mooladhara Chakra
Just below the base of the spine is the Mooladhara Chakra, which is the foundation of the whole spiritual 'tree of life'. Traditional

yoga charts often show a person sitting cross legged in the lotus position for meditation, and this is because the Mooladhara – and therefore the whole of the subtle system – benefits enormously from proximity to the grounding force of the earth. When we sit on the ground, the Mooladhara is in close contact with the Mother Earth which gives life to us all, through food, water and basic matter. It's no surprise then that this Chakra is affiliated directly with the Carbon atom, which is the primordial building block from which we are all made.

The main qualities embodied in this Chakra are innocence and wisdom, the bedrock of civilisation and the humanitarian lifestyle. We tend to equate innocence with naivety, but in fact the opposite is true. Real innocence involves a guiltlessness and a lack of motivated agenda, which is in fact very powerful. We see this quality most often in very young children, who act instinctively and without malice or premeditation. Wisdom implies that we are able to use our innate discrimination and subtle intellect to take the proper actions in every circumstance.

The qualities of purity and discipline are also a part of this Chakra and when all of these beautiful attributes are awakened through the cleansing power of the Kundalini we become very simple and yet deeply wise people. We lose our desire to play mind games, to indulge in complex and entangled relationships, and begin to enjoy the simplicity of a good, wholesome and deeply satisfying life.

Swadhishthan Chakra

Located at the point where the torso and the legs meet, this Chakra is the repository of our innate creativity. This centre, when nourished and cleansed, provides the well-spring from which comes the artistic creativity which is a hallmark of civilisation. We draw on the qualities and energies of this Chakra not only in our purely artistic endeavours, but also in any action that involves creative thought. So, for example, if we are called upon to make a creative decision at work or in our personal life, we will also be using the Swadhishthan.

The Chakra also embodies the ideals of eternal truth, or what we can think of as Divine knowledge. These truths – like honesty, compassion and peacefulness - are the foundation stones of civilised conduct, and are also signposts to the reality of God and the spiritual universe. We use the power of the Swadhishthan to help us identify and absorb the Divine messages on our spiritual journey. It is this Chakra that helps us recognise the truth behind the personal realisations we experience as we grow in our spirituality. In fact anything which hampers the flow of spiritual energy through this centre also impairs our ability to recognise the truth behind reality.

Nabhi Chakra

The Nabhi Chakra governs our sense of fulfilment. It is directly responsible for the amount of satisfaction we feel with our lives in a general sense. When this centre is in good order we experience an over-riding sense of peace. In a fundamental sense it can also indicate that we are nearing the end of our search for the spiritual truth, since our whole subtle system acquires a more settled aspect once this centre has been properly nourished by the Kundalini. The proper functioning of this Chakra is an essential component of our search for peace, as without a deep inner satisfaction with the condition of our life – however it may manifest – we cannot know peace and so progress in our subtle journey.

The Nabhi Chakra and the Swadhishthan both connect with our physical body on the right side through the functioning of the liver. Because the liver is the engine of our thoughts – it actually supplies glucose to the brain to feed our thought impulses – its subtle connection with the Nabhi has a direct affect on the quality of our thoughtlessness in meditation.

The condition of the Nabhi is therefore vital to our spiritual growth, which means that we need to pay special attention to the state of this Chakra (especially the Right Nabhi). Too much heat on the right hand channel – and the liver - can disturb our meditation and thus significantly interfere with our spiritual progress.

Heart Chakra

When we think of the heart, we think of love and of the organ which pumps vital blood around our body. In the same way the Heart (or Anahat) Chakra is an important part of our spiritual being, in that it is the home of our spirit (jivatman), a vital component of the individual's Soul. We often associate the heart with fear and bravery – e.g. being faint or lion hearted and suchlike - and so it is no surprise that this Chakra is also responsible for our personal sense of courage.

So it is no accident that our heart thumps if we receive a sudden shock. This is nothing more than a physical manifestation of the workings of the Centre Heart Chakra, which is responsible for keeping us stable, balanced and unafraid in the midst of unsettling or fearful circumstances.

Of course we also associate the heart with love and compassion, and it is at the level of the Heart Chakra that we learn the true meaning of compassion. When we talk of an open heart, we mean that this Chakra is completely open, allowing the full power of our pure spiritual love to pour out into our lives. This form of love is the most powerful energy in the universe, it is the source of Truth and the Divine light of existence. No wonder it has the ability to move mountains.

The Heart Chakra is also responsible for our sense of righteous duty or dharma, and it provides us with the firm resolve we need in order to act correctly in everything we do. When we are acting from unselfish and heartfelt motives we can do things that appear impossible. We only have to look at the incredible achievements of some of history's greatest heroes, such as Mahatma Ghandi and Dr Martin Luther King to see how this works.

Vishuddhi Chakra

This Chakra is the embodiment of our sense of community and humanity. It also helps us to get the best out of our relationships with others and lets us see things in proportion to their real importance. It is no accident that the Vishuddhi is located at the base of the throat, for that is the place which has most significance in terms of our communication with the world. It is through this communication that we build a sense of belonging and brotherhood one with another.

On the left side, the Chakra also is responsible for our sense of self worth. If we continually feel guilty, then we have all of our attention on our own failings which leaves us no time to reach out to others. Once the Left Vishuddhi has been cleansed we begin to understand just how important we are to the world and how much each of us can offer in our own unique and individual way.

As this centre becomes nourished we grow into more detached people, whose wise vision can calm the most troubled waters. Detachment does not mean we become cold or unfeeling. It is actually the most powerful form of compassion because it always acts for the best possible reasons, without us losing perspective. A detached and yet caring person will always find a way to soothe and counsel others, where someone who becomes too involved personally will find it hard to distance themselves from the situation.

Agnya Chakra

The clue to the power of the Agnya Chakra lies in its position at the centre of the forehead, for this is the centre which governs our thinking processes, and yet also allows us to ascend into deep meditation. Without the opening up of this Chakra our meditation is restricted, forced to remain locked at the level of the mind. But once this centre is fully opened by the Kundalini we can literally go 'beyond' the mind and achieve our real yoga in thoughtless awareness.

The Agnya responds to light and can only open fully when we have allowed the light of forgiveness to enter into our heart. By forgiving we leave behind the destructive thoughts which hold us down, and open out a whole new spiritual pathway to joy. It is for this reason that this centre can be one of the hardest to cleanse, and why many adepts traditionally spent decades working and working on the Chakra to try and rid themselves of mental obstructions such as anger, jealousy, lust, greed and other negative thoughts.

Sahasrara Chakra

The Sahasrara centre sits at the top of the head and is the pure synthesis of all the other Chakras rolled into one. This is the point at which we experience our true yoga and this is why the practice of Sahaja Yoga focuses so much on holding our attention at the top of the head throughout the meditation. Again it is no accident that this Chakra is located at the centre of the limbic area, where a thousand nerve endings from the physical body terminate. The subtle and the physical bodies are joined here in an intricately interlaced dance, which literally defines the state of our universe.

Once the practitioner's Kundalini passes through the Sahasrara, the process of yoga begins and the complete cleansing of the individual's subtle body gets underway. It is at this point that the adept learns the true meaning of the word silence. For yoga is ultimately nothing but silence. Eternal, infinite silence made real through meditation, devotion and dedication.

EFFECT OF THE CONDITION OF OUR CHAKRAS ON OUR DAY TO DAY LIVES.

Each of the Chakras has a direct and important role to play in our everyday lives. There is no such thing as a stable state for a Chakra, they are in constant flux, waxing and waning in strength and efficiency depending on our environment and our individual state of being.

These continual adjustments are also reflected in our physical state, as there are always direct correlations between the state of the Chakras and our physical well-being. Yoga adepts try to use this knowledge to correct problems before they become serious threats to their health, and use their meditation to maintain equilibrium between their physical and spiritual systems at all times. There are many different ways to identify imbalances in these systems, but here are a few of the clearest signs of a problem with our Chakras.

Mooladhara

The Mooladhara represents innocence and yet at the same time wisdom. As this centre begins to deteriorate, one of the first signs may be that our lives become more complex. Or at least appear to become so. Our memory may start playing tricks on us, we may find that everything we do becomes more difficult to accomplish and we become distracted by our obsessive focus on achieving material objectives.

At its most extreme level we can notice ourselves becoming sly, deceitful even, in order to manipulate our way to a goal. We can quite literally tie ourselves in knots, physical and mental, whilst trying to achieve some aim we consider to be important. And yet often in the end, the result does not give us any satisfaction at all, and so off we chase again in search of another unimportant goal to accomplish.

On the other hand, those with a strong Mooladhara Chakra exhibit the steadiness of a rock. They have personalities which are strongly rooted in truth and correct action, and they maintain a balanced lifestyle no matter how busy they may be. We often think of these people as 'steady' characters, reliable and trustworthy. They seldom exhibit the kind of doubts about action that many of us suffer from, and yet are caring enough to listen to all sides of an argument before making up their mind.

The way to help return to a balanced Mooladhara is to return to nature as our inspiration. Spend some time in nature, sit in silent meditation on the ground, or simply immerse oneself in the beauty of the natural world, flowers, grass, trees. Notice the details of life which are not man made, listen to the bird song, smell the flowers, enjoy the earth. After a time we will begin to regain our sense of perspective and start to appreciate the really important things in life, rather than the mundane.

Swadhishthan

A good sign that this centre is starting to move out of balance is when we start to have problems making decisions, or our decisions end up going wrong in one way or another. This Chakra is the centre of our creativity, but it is also the one which has direct connections to our thinking, planning and sense of truth. When it degrades, we end up suffering in all of these areas. We may start thinking and planning excessively, even to the point of exhaustion, as our attention is dragged from place to place, almost involuntarily.

We start to be consumed by self absorbed ambition, almost to the exclusion of everything else. We may even sacrifice real creativity for commercial goals, and so lose the ability to be spontaneously creative. We can even become dry personalities as a result. Hip pains, or pains in the nervous system such as sciatica may also indicate a weakened Swadhishthan. The left side of this Chakra reflects our ability to discern the truth when we come across it. Without it, we misread the signs and ignore those things that are beneficial for our spiritual ascent.

The individual with a strong and clear Swadhishthan on the other hand is often hailed as a genuinely creative person. They are praised for their humble approach to life and work, and are calm and collected as those around them go into a flap at the slightest provocation.

As with the Mooladhara, those with a strong Swadhishthan recognise truth and respect it above everything else. This type of personality will not be diverted from a 'correct' course of action because of external pressures or material desires. And above all they exhibit a real ability to make the right decision in all aspects of their lives, and especially when it comes to choosing wisely for their emotional and spiritual well-being.

An off balance Swadhishthan is restored to health by keeping our right side cool, using water during meditation to draw out the heat of over active thoughts, and by remembering during our meditation that ultimately we should surrender our actions to a spiritual goal. We can also help this centre by taking more care over what we eat, not over-burdening our liver with excessive quantities of pollutants such as alcohol, fatty foods or caffeine.

Nabhi Chakra

To be satisfied with all of the wonders of life is the hallmark of the Nabhi Chakra. Along with the Swadhishthan, this centre has a direct link with the liver, which is responsible for powering the thinking process of the brain. So the first symptom of the Nabhi centre going out of balance is the irritability and excessive thinking that comes from an over-active or hot liver. In its most extreme form we become compulsive worriers, about trivial, irrelevant matters that we believe are 'important'. A troublesome stomach or digestive system is also often a sign of a troubled Nabhi. We may even suffer from that quintessentially stress related ailment, ulcers of the stomach.

Those with a strong Nabhi seldom, if ever, complain about anything. They have a well defined sense of perspective about the relationship between their own well-being and that of the rest of the world . They know how to count their blessings and do! Their generosity also marks them out in a crowd, as does the fact that they seldom worry about money.

They seem to be able to overcome petty day to day worries by keeping their attention on things that are truly important, like generosity to friends, family and those who are in real need of help. In fact it is the left side of the Nabhi Chakra that houses our sense of family. Without a clear left Nabhi we may find it difficult to establish peace and harmony in our domestic surroundings.

A troubled Nabhi can again be helped through care of the liver, through eating properly, focussing on the important things in life rather than mundane materialism, and by counting up exactly how many blessings we do enjoy every day. We should also try and constrain any anger that comes from this 'liverish' imbalance, by

68

recognizing the artificial nature of this destructive emotion, and by remembering that deep down we are truly a spiritual and peaceful personality.

Heart Chakra

It is not merely romantic nonsense to say that the heart is the seat of our love and compassion. It is a fact. We open our heart to those that are closest to us both in a physical way (by demonstrations of affection and generous action) and in a subtle way through the feelings of tenderness and overwhelming concern we have for them. We say someone is closed hearted when they seem uncaring and selfish, and we call them open hearted when they give to all without question. These are real examples of the power of the heart to help or hinder our enjoyment of life.

A weak Heart Chakra can show up in many different ways, for example through mean spirited actions, or through deep insecurities which drive us to be selfish through fear. We can find evidence of a weak heart centre in those who are overly neurotic or frail, or in those who question everyone's motives. Even overly ascetic people can be victims of this problem.

In contrast the lion hearted fear nothing, are adventurous and derive more pleasure from giving than from receiving. They are unstinting in their praise of others and are the first to generously lend a hand when it is needed. They are also less likely to suffer significantly from general illness and disease, since they find it easier to resist the emotional uncertainty that can arise from the onset of an illness. You could say that they are simply hardier and more resilient to the kind of everyday ailments that put many of us in bed.

Vishuddhi Chakra

The Vishuddhi Chakra is a crucial contributor to our humanity. We use it everyday as we communicate with each other – no wonder it is situated at the base of the throat! It also governs our sense of respect, both for ourselves and for others. To 'have a chip on one's shoulder' indicates that we are unable to be generous to others, we think that the world is out to get us. In subtle terms those with a 'chip' are suffering from an ailing Vishuddhi which is out of balance, and which makes them feel cut off from the rest of the world.

Those who have a well nourished and clear Vishuddhi will be wonderful orators, and persuasive communicators of the truth. They will also exhibit a universal and gentle respect for everyone, regardless of job or station. For this reason they in turn command respect from others, and are often praised as having 'the common touch', meaning that they relate to all aspects of society, humble or grand. You will recognise someone with a strong Vishuddhi centre because they will be very soft spoken and yet at the same time authoritative. They will never have to raise their voice to display displeasure, and they will be firm of action since they do not carry around the traditional feelings of guilt or lack of self worth that are so common in the West.

Weakness in this centre is demonstrated by two contrasting features. On one hand you will see it in someone who constantly talks harshly of others, or complains loudly at every opportunity. Also those who belittle their colleagues, friends and family, or swear aggressively for no reason. On the other hand, a weakened left Vishuddhi can show up as false humility, a kind of crafty slyness that comes from a deep seated sense of guilt or inadequacy.

Someone with a blocked or weak left Vishuddhi on the left side will always focus on the negative aspect of a conversation relating to themselves and ignore any positive comments. No matter how much they are praised, they will remember only the time that they were criticised, even if it was justified. They will spend much of their time in a self-demeaning state of guilt, blaming themselves for problems which affect their own lives and others, even if it is not true.

We can help to repair and nourish this centre by adjusting our attitudes through diligent meditation. We can also use mantras –

incantations or invocations used to establish closer communication with the spiritual realm – to establish our sense of self-worth and remove guilt (e.g. 'I am not guilty'), and we can make an effort to practice the art of gentle and sweet communication with others at all times.

Soon we will stop complaining about things so much, and as we start to build a more positive attitude we will notice that this centre clears and we become more generous and comfortable in social settings. We make friends and keep them easier, we rarely find ourselves having to endure nasty arguments. The strong Vishuddhi defuses all potential trouble spots before they can flare up into something worse.

Agnya Chakra

A hugely important centre and one which plays a crucial part in both our material life and the rate of our spiritual ascent. The Agnya Chakra sits at the gateway to our yoga because of its proximity to, and relationship with, our brain and mind. This centre acts as a conduit for our thinking processes, responds to the demands of our ego and super ego and is the anchor that holds us captive in the material universe. It is only by transcending the Agnya and over-coming our mental concepts that we can enter into the true spiritual dimension and achieve union with the Cosmos.

A troubled Agnya gives rise to a frenetic thought process. We start thinking and thinking, we make plans, we become arrogant in our attitude to others. We begin to believe that only we have the answers and only we can do what needs to be done. The early sign that someone has a constricted Agnya is the fact that they exhibit an increasingly argumentative nature, they begin to argue with everyone over every little thing, even when they are clearly wrong.

As their problems with this Chakra progress they begin to slip into complete delusion, and can believe that they are supremely gifted, blessed or protected in everything they do, no matter how degraded. In its latter stages people can literally believe that they

71

have godlike powers over others, and that they cannot be stopped from doing whatever they wish. In physical terms, those with a constricted Agnya will often experience numerous headaches and sometimes shoulder pain.

Those with a problematic left Agnya (more usually termed 'back' to differentiate it from the 'front' Agnya) tend to suffer more from depressive or emotionally oriented problems, as well as other issues relating to their past and conditionings. They will be trapped by uncomfortable and deep seated 'issues' that may come from childhood or even past lives, and which make their life miserable.

A clear Agnya Chakra, on the other hand, is evidenced by a complete lack of pretension or aggressive ambition. Those with a balanced Agnya centre always try to listen to others, no matter what the situation. They will try and help where they can, and will avoid arguments in any form if they can.

Not only are they calm under pressure, but they actually become a beacon of strength in a crisis. They seldom rise to anger, and are quite content to surrender to a situation and see how it turns out. They cannot hold grudges and take great delight in enjoying the present moment wholeheartedly.

We can help our Agnya to stay clear and balanced by trying not to worry or think excessively. Our meditation will help us to touch the peace of yoga beyond the mind trap, but we can also help matters during our day to day activities by focussing on the present moment as much as possible. We do not need to dwell on the past or worry about the future, these are areas outside of our control anyway.

We can also help this centre by taking our attention away from the gross material world and onto the purity of nature as much as possible. A very important aid here is to forgive, and harbour no ill feeling towards any fellow human being.

Sahasrara Chakra

This centre is the point at which we move from the physical to the spiritual plane. We transcend the trappings of the human mind and move into a realm of peace and pure spiritual existence. This is the location of that famed state of Nirvana that has been written about for thousands of years. In practical terms this Chakra is the home of the faith we have in our spiritual progress, and so we need to maintain a strength of purpose in order to keep this centre clean and clear.

Someone with an obstructed Sahasrara will find it hard to relate fully to the beauty of any yoga or spiritual practice. They may even turn away from the concept of a Divine universe completely and become dry, cynical and sceptical individuals. As the doubts grow, their yoga too will begin to recede, until they fall back towards the atheistic illusion of materialism. Uncertainty, fearfulness and personal belief in the illusion of an isolated life are all hallmarks of this type of problem.

A clear Sahasrara is a giver of joy, peace and contentment. We can meditate on the peace within and fully experience the gentle power of our yoga. Because the head is the seat of all the Chakras integrated into one glorious whole, we experience a significant deepening of our experience of yoga when this centre is cleansed and the Kundalini is flowing through it unhindered.

THE INTEGRATED WHOLE

The subtle spiritual body is a miraculous, intricate and beautiful instrument. It exists in everyone from birth, dormant or semi-asleep, waiting for the opportunity to fulfil its potential and lead us to the reality of existence. It is the missing link in humanity's evolutionary progress, ignored and dismissed by science, vilified by religions and yet unmistakeably a Divine gift. Each of us has the freedom to ignore its call and continue to focus on the mundane and material world, or we can choose to follow the signs and make our way towards ultimate liberation.

For many of us, the choice is far from easy, accustomed as we are to putting our faith into things that can be seen, touched, smelled, heard or tasted. We may also be uneasy with new age idealism, tainted as it is with the wacky, bizarre and downright crazy fringe elements who dabble in nonsense and deceit. But above all we worry in case we're thought of as weird, as naïve losers with not enough sense to spot a phoney bill of goods when we meet it. We want to conform, be accepted and liked and not be judged and dismissed for foolishness.

The growth in the new age business and the proliferation of all colours and shapes of spiritual solutions has only made matters worse. It's not easy to trust again once you have been burned by a seemingly honest endeavour which turned out to be false. For these reasons, and many more, Sahaja Yoga is often also dismissed as nothing more than yet another yoga on the list.

There are, however, three simple but fundamental questions that we can ask, to learn whether a spiritual practice is true or false.

1) Does the practice aim to enslave you or set you free? Are you expected to labour as an apprentice for ever, or are you expected to become a real master of yourself and so liberate your true spiritual being?
2) Does it give you control over the whole of your subtle system? Not just a sensation here or there, or a limited set of spiritual powers, but a complete, interlocking and verifiable tool-chest of techniques and guidelines which deliver consistent results every time you use them?
3) Is it a business? Are you asked to pay money to progress in your spirituality? Is there a hierarchy of practitioners, and are you offered a document which claims to certify your ability?

These three questions point to the heart of any true yoga. Yoga is a natural, living process. It does not conform to modern commercial rules, no matter how attractively packaged. Unless the practice provides a slow, gentle and yet completely verifiable process of personal growth it is nothing more than an empty medicine bottle with a pretty label. Real yoga is not glamorous, nor easy. It does not seek out celebrity practitioners or try to glossily market itself to entice more followers. It is not trendy or fashionable, is not sold through smart advertising and smooth talking sales pitches, does not charge significant sums of money for progress to new levels of expertise, does not promise enlightenment for a fee.

Real yoga comes from the ancient forests of time. It is deferential, humble, quiet and hard working. It makes no promises and tells no lies. It has no quick, glib answers, nor does it sell itself with slick organisation and designer brochures. Real yoga is within you, locked in your subtle system, and when you find it, it is your success that is the triumph, not the form of yoga or the Guru that took you there. Self knowledge is the gift at the top of the tree, the ultimate personal achievement.

The subtle body is a miracle that belongs to all of us equally. We don't have to pay for it, beg for it or perform for it. All we have to do is desire it and be prepared to work, hard, to achieve its eternal promise. If we succeed, then we have done nothing more than fulfilled our true potential as a human being. If we fail, we will hurt no-one except ourselves.

– CHAPTER FOUR –

Meditation brings wisdom; lack of meditation leaves ignorance. Know well what leads you forward and what holds you back, and choose the path that leads to wisdom. The Lord Buddha

THE MEDITATION

There are many types of practice which can loosely be called meditation. At one end of the scale are the recreational forms, often accompanied by an artfully designed CD, video or matching book, or in some cases promoted via an electronic gadget or trendy new technique. These products serve a market desperate for a means of relieving the stress of modern living. Their job is to soothe the troubled mind, not spiritually, but mostly through some form of mental exercise.

In the middle are the quasi-religious practices, ranging from the eminently fashionable Zen-type meditations to those peddled for nothing more than commercial reward. Most of these practices are spiritual to the same degree as singing songs in a religious service, in that they offer a reasonable representation of spirituality without actually leading to any real spiritual liberation or evolution of the soul. They cannot, because they do not include the one crucial feature of all true yoga - self-realisation.

At the other end of the spectrum are the authentic forms of yoga meditation, as practiced by Seers for thousands of years. These practices have a genuine spiritual focus which overrides all other considerations, and they embody the crucial and timeless features of authentic spirituality, which have been documented over thousands of years.

76

i) Their core practice revolves around the authentic awakening of Kundalini energy through the process of self-realisation.

ii) They focus completely on overcoming the limitations of the body and the mind through the diligent practice of true meditation

iii) They are free of any material shackles such as money, ritual and organisation.

Anyone who seeks to achieve their complete spiritual awakening must seek out and pursue these objectives. If done properly, these spiritual practices transform the individual into a gloriously liberated being, free from material constraints and bathed in a complete understanding of their place in the universe.

Sahaja Yoga comes directly from this heritage, and stands at the crossroads between the more ascetically rigorous yoga of the past, and the needs of living in a modern age. On the one hand it focuses completely on the spiritual evolution of the individual through meditation, but it also offers a practical method of practicing the yoga whilst living a normal lifestyle. At its heart there are two key features – the awakening of the Kundalini, and the process of moving beyond the constraints of the mind into a spiritual state of meditation called thoughtless awareness.

The starting point for all Sahaja Yoga practice is the initial process of self-realisation. This event can happen anywhere and at any time, the only criteria being that it is accomplished through the assistance of a Sahaja Yoga instrument. This can be a photograph of Shri Mataji on a web page, a friend who 'gives' you your self-realisation or a visit to a Sahaja Yoga meeting anywhere in the world. How it happens is not really important, it is the effect and the long term consequences that matter.

Self-realisation, as we know from the earliest spiritual texts, is the ultimate goal for any seeker of truth and spirituality. It is the highest form of knowledge and enlightenment, and takes one beyond the mere physical world. To claim that Sahaja Yoga starts with this most profound of experiences may therefore sound far-fetched or even boastful, but this is in effect what happens.

The process of self-realisation begins and ends with the glorious awakening of the spiritual Kundalini energy inside each of us. Once this sacred female energy begins to flower and move from the base of the spine towards the top of the head along the central Sushumna channel, we are experiencing a true awakening into the spiritual dimension. However, this initial act is only the beginning of the total process of self-realisation. We then have to maintain our spiritual progress by continuing to meditate, to allow the Kundalini time to cleanse our subtle system and help us to grow and evolve towards ultimate enlightenment.

The goal of every Sahaja Yogi is to reach a state of enlightenment – the fourth or Turiya state – where we actually 'become' the meditation rather than just practice it. In this evolved state we are completely still and at peace with the world; thoughtless, connected and in a sublime state of awareness which is joy, knowledge and love. This is the destination, but between the start and the finish there can be many years of work to cleanse our system enough to allow this state to occur.

Sahaja Yoga can appear to be overly simplistic, as it seems to involve nothing more than sitting quietly. But in fact it's not like that at all, and behind the easy façade there's several thousand years worth of knowledge at work. However in the same way that we can turn on a light simply by flicking a switch, we can also make the process of meditation happen spontaneously, merely by giving ourselves the time for it to happen. Just by sitting down to meditate we encourage the Kundalini to rise from Her seat and do Her job.

At this point it should be noted that once the Kundalini has been awakened during the self-realization process that occurs during our first Sahaja Yoga meditation, She continually works on our subtle system, even when we are not directly sitting in meditation. But when we sit down to start a proper meditation session, She responds to our heightened desire and works more vigorously to provide a vehicle for our thoughtless awareness.

She acts as the cleansing agent during our meditations, the crucial key to allow us to progress, go deeper and touch the silence which is true yoga.

WHY DO WE MEDITATE?
Your vision will become clear only when you can look into your own heart. Who looks outside, dreams; who looks inside, awakes. Carl Jung.

The dictionary defines meditation as *'a devotional exercise of or leading to contemplation',* and nowadays when most people think of meditation they think of relaxing. In fact the idea of sitting down cross legged with eyes closed is universally accepted today as a sign of a peaceful state. However, the traditional purpose behind real yoga meditation was not to relax per se, but to achieve profound personal growth on a spiritual level.

Quite simply we meditate through yoga to achieve our release from the illusion of this material life. Everything else that occurs around and about that yoga – the peace, balance or self awareness - is a side benefit, something that we get as a result of our spiritual growth.

The word yoga means union or yoking, which refers to the union between our individual spirit and the universal Divine spirit. So how does this mystical union occur? Well, as we've seen in the previous chapters it happens through a subtle mechanism or energy called the Kundalini. The Kundalini is a conscious energy which exists in every person from birth, but usually in a dormant state.

Any student of Eastern philosophy or religion will know about this subtle spiritual system inside each of us, and the system of Chakras or energy centres which act as energy junctions. The Kundalini is simply the engine which makes the whole system work properly.

So when an adept is practicing yoga of any type, the end result must be to awaken the Kundalini energy and allow Her to cleanse, nourish and nurture the subtle system inside each of us. As this process occurs, the individual grows in self understanding and begins to take charge of their personal universe. Now whilst this may explain the mechanics of the yoga, it doesn't really explain the why – why do those who regularly practice this Sahaja form continue to commit a part of their busy schedules to meditation every single day?

Well, in simple terms we can say that we meditate to achieve three things;
    a) To heal and cleanse our subtle system
    b) To go deeper into our spirituality
    c) To experience a real and closer communication with God and the spiritual universe

Heal and Cleanse
Every time we sit down to do a Sahaja Yoga meditation, the Kundalini begins to rise up along the central Sushumna channel. She then starts the process of cleansing our Chakras, helping them to open and spin so that the energies inside us can flow more effectively around the whole subtle system.

This cleansing in turn allows the Kundalini an easier passage when she rises during the next meditation, and so on, so that we actually gain a cumulative benefit from the regular practice of meditation. Think of it as a snow plough clearing the road to make it easier for traffic to travel, which in turn makes it easier the next day for the plough itself to continue its clearing work.

Each of us is born 'inside' a physical body, along with a mind and a subtle system of energy flows. This subtle system is multi-dimensional in many different ways, and as we've seen, the energies that flow around it have a direct correlation to our whole being. Both the physical body and the mind are affected by the energy flows, because the energies also impact on our emotional trigger points like hormones and glands, as well as colour our perception of the world we see around us.

Now to ascribe all of this to invisible energy flows inside an invisible set of channels in an invisible subtle body may sound incredibly far fetched. After all, the medical profession rarely refers to anything other than physical and psychosomatic illness, and generally refuses to recognise any unconventional cause of ill health unless it has some link to well known genetic or environmental factors.

But there is an increasing amount of evidence which shows that it is not just physical triggers that are involved in a lot of the modern stress related problems. Scientists and broad minded medical practitioners are starting to uncover real evidence that we can cure or treat ailments through practices like meditation. For instance there are several studies around the world which show that regular practice of Sahaja Yoga can decrease blood sugar levels, reduce the incidence of migraine headaches and even alleviate some of the more severe symptoms of chronic asthma attacks. See *Sahaja Yoga Meditation as a Family Treatment Programme for Children with Attention Deficit-Hyperactivity Disorder,* [vii] as an example.

Regular meditation also has a beneficial effect on the Chakras which are linked to our physical nervous, hormonal and glandular systems. This means that the cleansing action of the Kundalini automatically helps to repair and maintain these crucial parts of the body. So, for example, we can often clear up a stomach ache simply by working on our Nabhi Chakra which is located in the area of the solar plexus. Or if we have a headache, we can reduce or stop it by holding a candle in front of the Agnya Chakra which is located in the forehead area.

Often a physical ailment is the result of not just one, but many different Chakras being affected, and so treatment will deal with all the different centres in unison. A good example of this are problems associated with the liver, which often can only be cured by cooling down the whole right side, as well as directly dealing with the Swadhishthan and Nabhi Chakras on the right hand side of the subtle body.

The key thing to remember about treating physical problems is that you need to be patient. We are accustomed to having instant remedies in this instant life, and so we can often feel cheated if something doesn't work within a few minutes. But in Sahaj terms, treating a problem will often take much longer than equivalent medicinal alternatives. This is mainly because Sahaja Yoga deals with the root cause of the problem, not merely the symptoms.

Sorting out a fundamental issue with our past, our conditionings or our lifestyle is a large task, even for the incredibly powerful Kundalini, so we shouldn't be surprised if fixing a deep seated problem takes a few weeks, months or even years. The thing to remember is that once a problem has been 'fixed' by our spiritual awakening, it stays fixed. No more repeat prescriptions. Which probably makes it worth waiting for!

So to recap, we meditate because it helps the Kundalini to rise, to cleanse the Chakras and improve the flow of spiritual energies inside us. We meditate to unload the accumulated 'junk' that we acquire each and every day from our modern, stress filled existence. We meditate also to compensate for our innate characteristic – be it left or right sided – which in turn helps us to become more balanced and more emotionally, psychologically and physically stable.

Finally we meditate to heal our long term imbalances, those which have grown up with us through childhood, adolescence and beyond. We really can change the type of person we are, drop the baggage we don't want and take control of our personality in ways that we couldn't imagine.

These then are the most direct benefits of the 'heal and cleanse' aspect of our daily meditation. It is important to repeat again that practising meditation simply to keep balanced is not the goal of our yoga. Otherwise we meditate in a vacuum. Our goal is to evolve into a complete and spiritually self aware being. We should treat the healing aspect of our meditation as no more than a side benefit of this improvement in our overall spirituality, and not let short term benefits obscure our long term objective!

Go deeper

It is because we meditate to evolve spiritually that we focus a great deal of attention on the process of going deeper. We call this 'going deeper' because it symbolises the sort of deeply peaceful and tranquil state which can be achieved through a Sahaj meditation. But there is more to it than just that.

To go deeper also means that we gain a greater understanding of ourselves and our universe. By doing this we become a more spiritual being, and detach ourselves more and more from the stifling restraints of a life focused on material things. In effect we become a meditative person, instead of merely doing a meditation practice.

This state, one of peace, equanimity and ultimately joy, is the supreme goal of any yogi. This self knowledge also helps us to re-discover our innate humanity. It is only by observing our negative attitudes, and flushing out our conditionings that we can really start to be ourselves. We can live life to the full without worrying about what others think of us, and perhaps most importantly we can start to revel in the freedom of innocence that comes from a pure enjoyment of life.

So how can we go deeper and what does it entail?

In basic terms, every time we meditate we try to reach a state of thoughtlessness. This is not a process of self-hypnosis nor is it a trance, but more of a search for complete stillness, where our thoughts subside significantly and we are at peace.

We all think. All the time. All sorts of thoughts, ranging from trivia to major events. The problem is that sometimes these thoughts threaten to take us over, we become edgy, unable to sleep and we suffer. By achieving a state of thoughtless awareness we can achieve emotional and spiritual balance, and allow the Kundalini to cross over the busy area of the mind at the Agnya Chakra where our thinking is focussed. If we can move beyond thoughts in our meditation, we can then experience true yoga, the union of the individual with the universal.

When we first learn to meditate it is almost impossible to slow down our thoughts, but over time – as more and more Kundalini rises to help us – we can experience a growing gap in the frequency of individual thoughts and touch that precious thoughtless state almost at will. We become adept at standing back during our meditation to watch the progress of individual thoughts as they enter and exit our mind.

One of the wonderful side effects of this state is the chance it gives us to introspect, to open ourselves up to the arrival of fundamental truths that can guide us in our amazing journey of self knowledge. These truths are called 'realisations', and they are a staple part of every yogi's life once they begin to meditate regularly.

Realisations are not the same as mental understanding. When we experience a new 'realisation' it is like uncovering a deeply held but long forgotten truth. The importance of these introspections and realisations cannot be overstated, and for many practitioners these realisations are vital signposts which show the way forward. They help us to lose our bad habits, to clarify confused situations and most importantly they provide crucial guidance as to the best direction to take for our future growth.

What form do they take? Well let's take an example. You may have been worrying about whether to stay in your job, and may have been compromising because of a fear of change. However during one meditation you may realise at some point - and that means truly realise, not just think about – that the job you have suits you perfectly, and that you're just going through a 'grass is greener' phase.

You will know that it is a realisation because it will come in the form of an absolute conviction, a fundamentally deep seated knowledge about a truth that you may have been avoiding or masking up till then. These are true realisations, and they are the building blocks of our growth, so we should treasure them.

The way to distinguish between a realisation and a mere thought is to see whether there is any uncertainty about the revelation involved. If there is, then you are still in the process of working out the problem. If there is no doubt that you have the right answer, if it 'feels' completely right down to the tips of your toes, then it is almost certainly a realisation.

Another result of our increased introspection through meditation is that we start to see the wood for the trees. Things start to fall into place and our perspective on life becomes much clearer in all ways. We begin to understand which things are truly important and differentiate them from stuff that we may have been clinging to out of fear or uncertainty. We also begin to lose our attachment to aspects of our lives that could have been holding us back in our personal growth.

Destructive relationships, conditionings, bad habits and a host of other baggage all eventually come under personal scrutiny during our introspections. We begin to see that money and the material aspects of our lives are not the most important parts of what we are and what we hope to become. But it's important to note that this is not just a mental process. Once these things become clear to us, we also have the power through meditation to take direct action, correct the situation and move on. We genuinely become our own guide and master.

Detachment sets us free, liberates us from fear, anger, destructive emotion and everything that can stifle our true selves. By examining ourselves through detached introspection we detect the real truth of our situation, and can laugh at the trivial whilst dealing with the important. We no longer feel guilty for our past or nervous about our future, we focus instead on enjoying the present moment as much as we can.

Another thing that we may notice as we meditate more is an improvement in the quality of our attention. Our attention is that part of our consciousness which we direct at specific things around us. When we are listening intently to something, we can say that we have our full attention on it. When we are focussed on looking at a small object, the same applies.

Our attention usually suffers in our day to day activities. It suffers because it is being pulled, jostled, screamed at, and battered by the world in which we live. As soon as we get up in the morning the breakfast television or radio starts screaming for our attention, with a stream of salacious news stories, beguiling adverts and a constant flow of general trivia. As we commute to work, seductive billboard advertising, newspapers or magazines vie for our attention, each trying to make us believe something or do their bidding. Shop windows scream out aggressive sales messages, offering come-hither blandishments and Final Sale, 50% Off! bargains in a thousand different attempts to attract our already battered consciousness.

This constant bombardment fractures our attention in a very subtle way. In fact we suffer more than we know, because after a while we lose the ability to settle down and find peace anywhere. One of the first signs is that we may have trouble sleeping, our mind racing with the events of the day. Eventually our attention becomes numbed by the 'noise pollution' and starts to demand increasing excitement; we may find that we get edgy unless we are doing things, that we get bored quickly and feel vaguely dissatisfied all the time, even when we're supposed to be having a fun time. Over a long period we can become desensitised to a normal lifestyle and actively seek out stress creating situations. We literally become excitement junkies. In children this is known as Attention Deficit

Syndrome, and in adults we call it a short attention span. Both are symptoms of the same thing, a worn out attention.

Our attention needs to rest in the same way that our bodies need to rest. The constant agitation of our mind through our senses can lead us to a remorseless and fruitless search for amusement and satisfaction in our lives. When we start to meditate, we begin to bring this aspect of ourselves under control. We cherish our attention, treat it with respect and help it to find peace wherever it can. It's like sending a young child to bed in the afternoon when they're tired but still excited. Eventually they learn to enjoy and be nourished by the peace, and thereby get more out of the remainder of the day.

In the same way, once our attention starts to calm down, it looks for more beneficial places to rest. Instead of being sucked in by loud visual and auditory inducements, it starts to enjoy the peace of nature, the gentle tones of a balanced existence. It seeks out tranquillity, and although it doesn't shun modern life at all, it leads us to the parts of our world which are most beneficial to our spiritual growth. Eventually we begin to generate our own peace from within, so that no matter how busy our environment, we remain in a state of calm and balance. This is where the power of real yoga starts to act directly on us, as we literally become the meditation.

As we go deeper, we also become adept at listening to the needs of our attention, and eventually learn how to use it to interact more dynamically with our world in a positive way. We seek out beauty and feed on it, and in turn our spirit is nourished by the new and rewarding menu.

It is a sad fact that much of the turmoil that comes from living in the modern world starts with the damaged attention of the young. If we could learn at an early age how to cherish and protect this most precious of assets, our lives could be so much better in so many ways.

87

So to sum up, going deeper in our spirituality is a marvellous journey of discovery, which brings tangible benefits and a real sense of achievement to our lives. It is also essential for us if we are to progress at all in any meaningful way as a spiritual person.

Enjoy a spiritual communion

One of the eternal questions of humankind, perhaps the most fundamental question, is whether we exist alone? Is there any other entity or universe which we cannot see, but which nonetheless exists? Is there a God, a creator? These are the mysteries of life, and it is on these questions that all religions have focussed.

However as we grow into adulthood we often learn that these questions are not compatible with living the type of 'successful' modern life that is expected of us. The magic of existence is quite simply knocked out of us at a very early age, and we are forced to 'conform' to the norms of society. We must work hard, pass exams, get a good job, earn a living, settle down, build security, not rock the boat, enjoy our retirement, grow old gracefully, and finally exit our world with dignity and a few savings.

No time for existential thought, no point either because we're never going to prove anything one way or another. In the face of this subtle but inexorable pressure most of us take the easy option. We conform. We bury all of our innocent childlike belief in God and in the innate goodness of the world, and settle down to a regimented form of conventional thought. We pay lip service to our vanishing spirituality by establishing ourselves as part of a religion. We become a 'Christian', a 'Hindu' or a 'Jew', 'Muslim' or 'Buddhist'. Or even an atheist.

We travel along the safe road, one which our friends, partners and colleagues are comfortable with, and one which puts us into a convenient little box with a label which says, 'I may not believe the same as you, but at least you can understand where I'm coming from'. But deep down, in our innermost beings, most of us retain at least a little bit of that childlike faith in the glorious possibility of the spiritual dimension. We have a nagging feeling that our sterile 'belief system' is not the real thing at all; these fragile religions with their dogma, their fallible leaders and their all too human frailties.

Some of us rebel completely and may even go off in search of the 'real truth'. We become seekers, because deep down we KNOW that there's more to it than church on Sunday, prayers on Friday or a book of rules and some incense. Traditionally the seekers after truth have always trudged towards the East, weary, downcast but ever hopeful that one day they would meet THE ONE who would explain it all, or that they would experience for themselves the enlightenment written about in the ancient texts.

For the rest of us, however, life moves on in a safe, predictable and structured fashion. But if you're reading this book, chances are that you're curious about the possibility of breaking out of the cage. You have decided perhaps to have one more try at rediscovering your childlike enthusiasm for life, to locate a real God as you have always suspected, or hoped, existed. You're reading this to see if there really is a way to prove that life is not as empty as the washing powder ads would have us believe.

The good news is that an answer does exist. Oh, it's not as glib as you'll find in those cleverly marketed books by authors with hollow smiles. The ones which explain so persuasively what and why you are, and what to do/eat/feel/think in order to improve your condition. There are a lot of those books around - self help, improvement, spiritual-food-for-the-soul type books. They satisfy us for the length of time it takes to read them, and then – like some cosmic junk food meal – the insubstantial words begin to fade away from our consciousness, and we slip back once again into the drudgery of modern life and its pressures.

It's like reading the prescription on a bottle of medicine. We can read it time and time again. We can understand the words, relate to the sentiments, recognise the truth of the advice. But until we take some actual medicine we are never going to get better. In a somewhat bizarre twist, you are reading a book which suggests that you stop reading books. Move on, do the yoga, become the yogi, stop prevaricating and change yourself and the world around you.

So why do we meditate? Probably the single most important reason is to establish, nurture and enjoy a tangible and continuous relationship with the reality of God. We establish a real communion with the spiritual universe, in which everything takes on a powerful and symbolic significance. Every action, inaction, thought, word and deed. We see the Divine play in every second and atom of existence. We frolic in the knowledge that we are no longer alone, that we are being looked after in every single way.

Of course the price we pay is the return of responsibility. We understand that there is a consequence to all of our thoughts and deeds. But instead of turning into chains, this responsibility liberates, as we explore a world where the magical is commonplace. We relish the freedom that comes from recognising where we fit into the universal play of life. We relax as we understand the nature of the ultimate goal of life and its infinite message.

Now to many this may seem totally far-fetched. To others it may look like an overblown extension of the ritualised belief of the traditional religions – 'follow us for we know the truth about God'. But there is a difference, and it's a key difference. In a traditional religion, the adherent is expected to take it on trust that a Creator exists. The deal is that if we practice our religion with a good heart, we will be rewarded at the end of our lives with a place in heaven, a seat in Divinity.

A Sahaja Yogi goes beyond this basic belief system into a universe of absolute knowledge and experience. Every day brings a direct proof of the divine communion in action! Practicing a true yoga does not involve any blind belief of any kind, except perhaps at the very beginning when the process starts to crank into action. In the very early days of our meditation we may not feel very much at all, and it is at this point that we are most vulnerable to doubts and negative persuasion.

It is a fact that most people – perhaps 8 out of 10 – fail to make it past the first few weeks of their early meditation practice before giving up for one reason or another. Either they lose heart when they fail to notice any appreciable difference in their lives in the first few days, or they find it difficult to set aside the time to meditate. Or they simply don't have enough will-power or patience to stick at the practice.

Those who persevere and maintain a steady practice do however reap the rewards. Just as patience and diligence can help you in any endeavour, so it is with real yoga. Dedicated practitioners of Sahaja Yoga begin to experience a tangible communion with their own spirituality on many different levels.

On the most basic level, they will notice that the world takes on a more significant dimension. Messages and clues are dotted around waiting for those who want to see, and these begin to manifest in very direct ways as we continue to meditate. These clues are absolutely personal, and therefore differ markedly from person to person, which makes them all the more recognisable.

At first we may believe them to be coincidences, serendipitous events. However pretty soon it becomes clear that there are just too many chance meetings, spiritual conversations, significant events pointing in the same direction to pass them all off as coincidental. We may pick up a discarded newspaper on a train seat and read about the new power of love to calm the spirit and remove stress. We may find ourselves talking long into the night with our boss about spiritual matters. We may pick up a book at random in a library and read a direct answer to a question that has been troubling us.

A million different and astonishing manifestations of this sort can present themselves to us as we begin the journey, and it is up to us to recognise them and learn from them. They are there to show us that we do not embark on this journey alone, nor do we do it randomly. There is a loving and helping hand very close by to lend assistance as and when we need it.

After a while we begin to look out for the signs and to relish their presence. They vary enormously in intensity, volume and message from person to person and period to period, but they are a constant companion to those who meditate in yoga. Thus, over time, we build up a knowledge of the truth that goes beyond belief, that relies on tangible signals to guide our way.

Vibratory awareness

Surely all devout people have this connection with the Divine though, you may ask. And to a certain extent this is very true. Prayers have been known to produce many miracles down the ages, and they have been documented in all types of religions. However the biggest difference between communication done through simple prayer and that done through the yogic connection of the Kundalini, is that with the yoga we have a new awareness which proves that our divine conversation is two way, rather than a one sided question of faith.

The vibrations that we feel, the soft gentle breeze-like coolness we feel flowing across the hands, head or body, provide us with incontrovertible proof that we are in conversation with the spiritual dimension. This is known as vibratory awareness, and it is one of the cornerstones of Sahaja Yoga meditation. Vibrations are nothing less than the play of spiritual energies around our physical body, in a controlled and verifiable form.

Once the Kundalini has been awakened, we gain an extra 'sense' as it were, which can feel the flow of energies as this cool breeze or light wind. It can be very subtle, although many people are still quite startled when they first experience the flow, and look around for an open window or air-conditioning system. However these vibrations are real, and they serve to give us a sense of direction, communication and feedback from the spiritual realm.

We use them to work on ourselves and with each other in our meditation workshops. They are used to identify the truth behind a situation or issue. We can feel them flowing strongly where there is love, purity or a Divine environment of some kind. We feel the lack of them – a sort of heat or prickling sensation on the hands or body – where we are in a hostile, aggressive or harmful setting which is potentially damaging to our spirituality.

This is pure divine communication at its most direct, and it is definitely not self suggestion or hypnosis. There have been many, many instances of practitioners of Sahaja Yoga feeling some form of vibrations without any idea of its meaning until after the event. Walking past a place without knowing that it is the home of a saintly person and feeling cool sensations on the hands as the Vibrations responded. Meeting someone who is ostensibly nice, but who emits unpleasantly warm vibrations, and then is later found out to be fraudulent. The examples are legion!

After a while, the yogi starts to rely on these vibrations in all activities, although eventually, as we go deeper in our spirituality, the 'message' from the vibrations changes to an overall 'sense' of a situation, rather than just a flow of cool or warm. However in the early days, it can be an intensely exciting and rewarding experience to experiment with our growing vibratory awareness in different circumstances – and many eager newcomers to the practice do so enthusiastically.

Can we say for sure how it works, or why it happens as it does? The answer is no, not really.

We know that the Vishuddhi Chakra at the base of the neck has a direct affect on our ability to feel the flow of vibrations. Those who have been heavy smokers in the past often have the most difficulty feeling vibrations at first, at least until the Chakra becomes cleansed. And we know that the vibrations can occur at the most unexpected times, often when we're least expecting them.

Whatever the reason, we know that vibrations work, and work well. We trust this new perception because it proves time and again to be an astonishingly accurate form of communication, even when repeatedly tested against the practitioner's personal prejudices, conditionings and temperament. For example, often there will be a situation where the vibrations indicate to us that a particular course of action is not going to be good for us, but our ego disagrees. So we proceed anyway, and then learn the lesson when the results turn out to be less than satisfactory. If this happens once, it could be a coincidence, but again and again in different circumstances and places? So this is not blind faith or belief, but a real and verifiable stream of communication which works at a subtle level for all those who keep their Kundalini fully awakened through meditation.

This awareness and communication is also hugely valuable as a method of improving our self-knowledge. We can use it to identify important facts about ourselves, our environment and even our weaknesses by 'asking' the vibrations to indicate the truth. Should we take this job, how can we improve our relationship, is this offer genuine and beneficial? We can ask the question to ourselves, and see whether we feel cool or heat on our hands. We can even write down the questions, shuffle the papers and see if one note is 'cooler' than the other in a blind test. There are many different ways to take advantage of this amazing new sense.

The important thing to remember about the use of this new relationship, however, is that it is based around one thing – our spiritual benevolence. Often we can receive a response to a query that does not fit in with the facts as we see them at all. Sometimes the vibratory answer may not even make sense. It is only after we have taken action – whether in agreement with the advice given or not - that we will learn why. In some cases this education can be years in coming.

For example, a job that we thought was perfect for us, especially in material and security terms, may be harmful for us in terms of our spiritual ascent. It may be too stressful to allow us to meditate properly, or too hostile an environment. When it comes to a tussle between the material benefits of this lifetime and the spiritual benefits of our eternal ascent, the vibrations will always point us towards the latter.

One of the main challenges in using this vibratory sense, is to recognise, trust and surrender to its benevolence, even where we may not understand the advice. This, it has to be said, is probably the most difficult aspect of any yogi's practice. It doesn't matter whether you're young or old, or have been practicing for 5 minutes or 50 years, surrendering to the benevolent desires of your spirit can be a very difficult thing to do.

And yet the irony is that when we do, in every case things work out perfectly in the end. The frustration for many is that waiting until 'the end' can tax our patience to the limit. The Divine does not work according to impatient human timescales, and the wait for a benevolent resolution to a human problem may take years of meditation, cleansing and dedication. But such is the nature of this glorious journey.

So why do we meditate? Well, to evolve, to perfect ourselves, and to fulfil our complete and rightful potential as a spiritual human being. Is the journey easy? No. The start may be effortless, but then the work begins. The Lord Buddha on his deathbed exhorted his followers to '*be diligent*', and nowhere is this more true than in following our yoga as he did. We meditate to find love, peace and truth. We meditate to fulfil our purpose in life. This is why we are born.

HOW TO MEDITATE
There is no one method of meditation that fits everyone, and in fact our meditation will change shape many times throughout our yoga journey, as we address different issues in our spiritual ascent.

We may start off needing to spend time cleansing a particular subtle area, and then after a few months, or even years, find ourselves concentrating on other areas which need attention. This is a continual process and a lifetime quest, so we shouldn't expect to do exactly the same format of meditation every time we sit down. There is, however, a definite structure to a Sahaja Yoga meditation, and understanding how it works will help us gain maximum benefit from the practice from day one. The following suggestions are therefore aimed at helping newcomers who wish to establish an easy to understand routine early on.

In simple terms we meditate by sitting silently with our attention inside. The mere act of taking time out for ourselves, to sit silently and move our focus away from external distraction, is a form of meditation in itself. However after our Kundalini has finally been awakened, this quiet introspection becomes a more dynamic process, as we establish a real contact with our inner spirit.

Before starting

First, find a place in your home where you can sit comfortably without being disturbed, preferably a location that can be used regularly. It is not necessary to sit on the ground, you can use a chair or sit anywhere as long as you are comfortable. Try to remove any potential distractions, for example by turning on the answering machine before you start. It helps to have a lighted candle in place in front of your position, along with a small photograph of Shri Mataji which you can use as a focal point to help you relax. The photograph emits strong, soothing vibrations and along with the powerful cleansing action of the candle makes it easier to slip into a meditative state.

Those meditating for the first time may find it difficult to sit still or take their attention inside as they close their eyes, but this does get easier with practice, and there are a couple of simple tricks we can use to help make it easier to go into meditation. For example, if we are feeling overly agitated, just sitting quietly in a not too bright room or a shady location outside can help to cool down our right side energies and move us a little more into the centre before we start. Similarly if we are feeling out of balance through being a little depressed or tired, we can improve matters by sitting in a well lit room or in the sunshine for our meditation.

We can think of meditation as having three distinct stages;
1) The Settling
2) The Clearing
3) The Stillness

Settling

Once we are seated, we can raise our Kundalini and put ourselves into Bandhan as per the instructions we have been given in our local Sahaja Yoga weekly meeting (or see Appendix B). We can then sit with our eyes closed and hands outstretched on the lap with the palms upwards, and move our attention slowly from the base of the spine to the top of the head. At this point we can use the affirmations we learned in the meeting to help us gently take our attention inside, or if we have not yet had the chance to attend a meeting we can simply say to ourselves silently *'please may I go deeper into meditation'* a few times.

After a few moments we may feel tingling, cool or heat on our fingers or a slow, gentle ripple of movement along the spine as the Kundalini starts to rise from the base of the spine to the top of the head. It helps if we try and ignore these sensations to start with – and don't worry if you don't feel anything, as everyone's experience of meditation is obviously different – since we are trying to achieve a state of thoughtlessness, where we are not dragged along with our thoughts, but simply watch them slowly float into and out of our consciousness.

This early stage of the meditation is the part which can be the most frustrating, where the thoughts pile into our minds unbidden and unwanted, and we start to react. This is the point at which we really need to detach ourselves, not become discouraged and just allow the Kundalini to rise slowly from her base. The thoughts are bound to come in a rush once we close our eyes, because our mind is still working at full pelt processing the data from our senses.

After a short time, once the Kundalini has started opening and cleansing the Chakras, we will notice a slowing of the thoughts. This first stage of our meditation is like the prologue to a book, or the opening musical overture of an opera. We need this time in order to allow our thought processes to unwind, and so it shouldn't be rushed and we shouldn't become frustrated because we think that it's not working.

One thing that can be very helpful at this stage is to try and balance our subtle system, either by cooling down our right side or heating up our left side. By using the relevant technique at this early stage we can help the progress of the Kundalini up through the central channel and ease our transition into a deeper meditation.

Many people report that this is the time when they feel the Kundalini flowing up their spine most strongly, creating cool vibrations around the body. This is because it is at this transition point that we are most sensitive to the changes in our subtle state that occur. At the start of our meditation session the Kundalini surges to the top of the head and having reinforced the link to our yoga at the Sahasrara Chakra, pulsates with greater intensity inside the subtle body to continue the cleansing process.

After a few moments we may notice that our breathing has slowed a little, and that external sounds, although still audible are receding from our attention. After a few years of meditating we may notice that this transition into a detachment from our surroundings takes less time to manifest and is much more intense. In effect we create a spiritual 'bubble' inside which our meditation takes place.

Eventually we actually become this bubble and take it with us wherever we go, which is a marvellous part of the whole Sahaja Yoga experience. In the early days, however, most of this first part of the meditation will generally be taken up with trying to soothe down our attention whilst moving it gently inwards.

At this point we don't really need to think about actively clearing our subtle system through the use of any techniques, we can just enjoy for a while before the next stage arrives.

Clearing

After a few minutes we may notice that while we are sitting more peacefully, thoughts are still flowing through our minds. This is quite natural and we shouldn't think that the meditation isn't working simply because of this continued thinking. Just bring our attention slowly back to the top of the head and try to keep it there. In fact it will take quite a bit of practice before we are likely to notice a significant slowing of the flow of thoughts, but we will experience the benefits of our meditations long before that time.

Fig 2

The clearing stage is the point at which we help the Kundalini along in Her work. We do this by using our attention to focus on our energy channels, Chakras and mental activity. At the same time we can use any of a number of techniques to help cleanse our system and allow more Kundalini through, although we should remember that the real work is not being done by the technique itself, but by the desire of our attention.

For instance we may feel lethargic one morning, and decide in the clearing stage that we need to work on our left side to help the energy flow more freely on that side. We can do this by moving the

99

energy of the right hand channel across to the left side with our right hand, up and over 108 times.

We can also continue to clear the imbalance by pointing our right hand towards the floor for a few moments (or by resting it on the floor if we are sitting on the ground). (see Fig 2 above)

We should start feeling the benefit of this after a few minutes, but in extreme cases we may decide that we need to go even further and cleanse the Ida Nadi (left side channel) by strategically placing one or more candles adjacent to the left side of our body, taking care with the naked flames of course. There is a very effective treatment for depression and lethargy of the left channel called the Three Candle Treatment, ask at your local meeting for details. We can also carefully and slowly move a candle up and down the front line of our left channel from waist to shoulder to cleanse the channel more effectively.

Fig 3

Conversely we may feel too 'speedy' and full of thoughts, so to wind down and go into a more balanced state we can move the energy of the left channel up and over into the right channel 108 times again using our right hand. Again we can continue this clearing by holding the left hand up in the air to vent the heat from the over-heated right side. (see Fig 3)

These are perfectly standard techniques in Sahaja Yoga, but we must remember that their effectiveness comes directly from the power of our attention, rather than from our physical actions. The heat from the candle is actually empowered by our enlightened attention to cleanse our left side, and it is actually the subtle desire of our attention which transfers the positive energy of the right over to the left, and so on.

This is why it is important that we employ these techniques with full confidence, focus and respect! If we practice our meditation half heartedly, even though we may not be experiencing as much as we had hoped, then we are short changing ourselves. We are not giving our enlightened attention the chance to work out our problems as efficiently as it could.

Of course every time we sit down to meditate, our desire triggers the meditative process automatically and cleansing occurs, but it is so much more effective if we put our full attention behind it. Like everything else in life, you definitely get out of Sahaja Yoga what you put in. This doesn't mean that we should become fanatical, just sincere in our desire to grow. That's why it's probably better not to spend too much time working on ourselves during the meditation. If we spend at most a third of our whole meditation on clearing the blockages in some way, we will have done more than enough.

In fact it is the final stage of our meditation, where we simply sit in silence and try to sustain a peaceful, thoughtless state, which delivers the most important benefits of our yoga.

Clearing techniques
The left side: The left channel is our moon side, the feminine side of us which represents our desires, emotions and past. As such it is considered to be the cool side and can affect us by making us feel depressed, lethargic, introverted and self pitying. So to clear it, we use the primordial elements of light and heat:

* Sit in a light place or take a little sun occasionally, especially to the back of the head.
* Use 3 additional candles arranged around the left side of the body when meditating.
* Place a lighted candle near to the outstretched left hand when meditating.

101

* Slowly and carefully move a lit candle up and down the left side of the body during the clearing part of the meditation using the right hand. This will gently and subtly cleanse the channel and restore balance to that side.

* Try to avoid excessive daydreaming about the past.

* Try and eat more protein, and avoid carbohydrates as much as possible without being over zealous.

The right side: The right channel is the sun side, the masculine side of us which represents our action, planning and the future. It is therefore susceptible to over heating, which can easily throw us off balance. If we find that we have suddenly become more aggressive, unsympathetic or stressed then we may be suffering from an over heated right channel. To clear the right side we use the power of physical coolness and avoid too much heat or brightness:

* We should avoid hot temperatures and situations and bright sunlight for a time. Enjoy a little time spent in the moonlight at night if possible.

* Footsoak during the evening meditation by placing both feet in a bowl of coolish water containing a sprinkling of household cooking salt.

* Eat less protein and try to increase the intake of carbohydrates. Cane sugar is a very effective coolant for the right side, as is yoghurt in the summer.

* Try to avoid excessive planning and other futuristic actions.

* If possible have a short rest at least once a day.

The liver is connected to our subtle right side and is adversely affected by over heating. A good method of cooling the liver is to place a cloth covered plastic ice pack (or ice cubes wrapped in a plastic bag and dry dish towel) onto the liver area on the right hand side of the body (just under the ribs) during the meditation. It should be cold enough to be felt without being uncomfortable.

If the problem is more persistent consider using the Liver Diet (see Appendix D)

Stillness

The final stage of our meditation is where we try to settle into a tangible zone of peace and stillness within and around ourselves. This zone should feel remote from the noise, smells and sensations around us, and yet we should still be completely alert and aware. There are bound to be some distractions, unless we're lucky enough to be meditating on a remote mountain top, but nevertheless, with practice we should be experiencing a bubble of peace in which we can sit without thoughts.

The idea is that having taken our attention inside, we can now detach ourselves from the future and the past, and simply watch our consciousness as it drifts in and out of thoughtless awareness. It is almost impossible for us to completely stop the flow of thoughts, instead our goal is to slow them down to a lazy crawl. Indeed, after we have been meditating for some months we may notice that the volume and intensity of thoughts in this later crucial stage of our meditation has reduced significantly.

There is a point to note.

If this final stage of the meditation is still mentally very busy, it may be that we need to look at the general state of our right side and/or liver in more detail. It may be that we are in a period of intense stress which is making our brain super active and therefore making it hard to reach the quiet state. In this case we can take steps to correct this phase as mentioned above. We can also take care with what we eat, and avoid fatty fried foods, heavy red meat and anything else that may 'heat' up our liver.

On the other hand, if we can't sustain the stillness because we're too tired or lethargic, we can try to keep ourselves in a more upbeat frame of mind by focussing on the positive aspects of our lives, and trying to avoid anything or anyone likely to pull us down in any way. We can avoid over using depressants such as alcohol, and try and keep active to compensate for our lethargy.

We can also try and keep our attention in check in general, by making a conscious effort to check the deluge of thoughts, even in our daily activities. It's surprising how therapeutic it can be to slow down every so often, pull back from whatever we are doing, and move our attention to the top of the head to slow down our thoughts. It also provides a sort of training for the mind, which over time helps us to go into meditation easier.

The stillness may not be an easy place to find, nor re-visit, as it requires our diligent desire and yet at the same time cannot be forced. The main thing that we can do, however, is avoid rushing things. We should try to allocate enough time to our meditation so that we can relax into this final golden third period and experience this peaceful space in whatever form it comes.

Unfortunately people sometimes find their meditation to be more of a chore than a pleasure, something that 'has' to be done, rather than something which they look forward to doing. This can come about because they find it difficult to give themselves enough time to reach this final enjoyable stage, and so they short change themselves each time they meditate. Of course the Kundalini does not care what point we reach in our meditation, Her role continues every time we sit down to meditate, no matter how long or short it is.

Nevertheless it is probably fair to say that this section of the meditation gives us the most powerful rewards in every way. The quality of the final stage of the meditation can make the difference between us finishing up refreshed, light and ready to take on the day, or with nagging thoughts still hovering in our attention.

We seek to establish balance and healing in every meditation, and most of this is achieved in the final third part of the session as the work of the Kundalini intensifies, and She focuses on strengthening our Divine connection. It is during this phase that we are also likely to touch the inherent joy of the spirit, as the peace inside us grows. All the more reason not to waste the opportunity by rushing things!

Finishing up

Once we have finished meditating we can slowly and gently end the session. The meditation is completed by our raising our Kundalini again and putting on a Bandhan exactly as we did when starting off. If possible we should try and rise slowly, and not in a rush to leave the home or start a new task. We have been in a special place for our meditation, it is a mark of our gratitude and respect that we leave it slowly and with dignity.

If we have been to a great party, do we rush to the door when it's done, scramble into our coat and run to the gate? Or do we linger, savouring the occasion for a while longer and take our leave gently with love and thanks? Why should it, then, be any different for our experience of meditation?

WHEN SHOULD WE MEDITATE?

Ideally we should aim to meditate twice a day, morning and evening. It is important to try and establish a regular routine in this way, rather than meditating in irregular bursts, because this helps the cumulative cleansing action of the Kundalini to work best. Every time we meditate we not only cleanse our system and bring ourselves into a more balanced state, but we also prepare and condition our subtle system ready for the next meditation.

If we miss a meditation, we make the subsequent one more difficult, as the Kundalini has to work harder to cleanse and correct the additional imbalances. Nor is it advisable to miss a few days and then try and meditate for longer to make up for it. There is only so much that we can get out of any single meditation, and if we try to force things by meditating for an excessive length of time, we risk going out of balance either on the left or the right side.

Steady and often is best.

The morning meditation is important to set us up for the day. It tends to be a longer meditation than the evening one, and should ideally be as simple as possible. We are trying to bring ourselves into balance to face the day with our full powers, so at the very least we need to experience a short period of thoughtless awareness during which our Kundalini is operating at Her peak.

We also use the morning meditation to strengthen ourselves in more fundamental ways. We may, during the deepest part of our morning meditation, experience startlingly important realisations about our environment, relationships and life in general. These are key milestones on our spiritual journey, and so should be cherished. It is probably fair to say that the majority of our spiritual growth occurs during this meditation, and although both of the daily sessions are important, this one is not to be missed if at all possible.

The morning meditation, however, is often the first victim of our erratic schedules or over-sleeping; it can be so much easier to leave out the morning yoga than skip breakfast or risk missing the bus. In fact, this meditation is vital for our long term well-being because it grounds us and helps us withstand the stresses and strains of each day. Without it we enter the modern world wearing only half of our armour, and loosely buckled at that. With the meditation done, we are properly clothed, ready to take the stresses and strains of the day as they may fall.

One of the easiest ways to overcome the time problem is to hitch up our determination and wake up earlier, even if this means going to bed a little earlier. In most instances any action we take like this tends to be temporary anyway, because we soon develop a more comfortable sleep and meditation pattern as we progress in our practice. But in the early days it can be difficult to fit in our meditations between dressing, eating, bathroom and train schedules.

It may help to remember that while we often lavish more time on getting ourselves dressed and ready in the morning than on our meditation, only one of these activities is a crucial part of our eternal spiritual liberation. Guess which?

106

The evening meditation is a much gentler affair, more soothing and one which we use to remove the debris of the day. We accumulate subtle spiritual pollution every day; from our workplace, colleagues, from events, circumstances and even chance encounters. Negative vibrations, imbalanced personalities, hostile spiritual energies and the like. This rubbish wears us down and is harmful to our general state of balance in many different ways.

We can use our evening meditation to clear away this negativity and refresh our subtle spiritual system. Arguments, confrontations, fears, insecurities and stress are all things that can be washed away incredibly effectively through the use of footsoaking and meditation. We footsoak by placing our feet in a bowl of lukewarm, lightly salted water. The salt represents the earth, and along with the fire of the candle and the water, represents the power of the primordial elements which we use to help cleanse our subtle system.

This evening meditation is when we can spend a little time working on ourselves, clearing our Chakras, using the elements to cleanse a blocked left side, or cool an overheated right side. We can use mantras in a more focussed and prolonged way and perhaps even listen to some soothing spiritual music – try a little Indian classical sitar or flute - or a talk by Shri Mataji to help our vibrations flow more efficiently. You can obtain such talks from your local Sahaja Yoga meeting.

Meditating regularly in the evening helps to soothe down our thinking process so that we sleep more soundly. It lets us relax properly in a way that a 'stiff drink' seldom achieves. We emerge from the session alert, refreshed and in balance; the events of the day a distant memory. It is this meditation, therefore, that helps to build our overall sense of detachment and reduce any emotional turmoil. It also sets our system up for a good night's sleep and cleanses the subtle system ready for a more invigorating meditation the next morning.

Sometimes there may a temptation to skip the evening session, especially if we return home late and exhausted – '*I'm just too tired to meditate properly*'. Indeed we may even start to meditate and find ourselves nodding off to sleep as we do so. This is very commonplace and often people just give up and go to bed. This is a real shame, because if we resist the temptation to given in and instead continue to meditate, we take a very important step in winning control of our body, and therefore our lives.

If we allow ourselves to be dominated by concepts of sleep, tiredness and the like then we are in fact slaves to our body. This idea of tiredness is very much a mental concept rather than a fact, which can easily be proved. How many times have we returned home 'dog tired' and ready for bed, only to receive a very pleasant surprise in one form or another? A present, a windfall, a visit from a dear friend or relative? Immediately we are alert again, as our mind and then body respond to the pleasant stimulus.

The physical cause may indeed be a rush of adrenaline or other chemical reactions, but these are triggered by the mind, and so we know that they come from a mental state. If we can recognise that our tiredness is simply a reaction to a conditioning, then we can fight it by deliberately meditating even though we may feel desperately weary. Even if we nod off during the session, the fact that we have started means that the Kundalini begins Her work and we receive the benefit.

A very useful technique to help us stay awake is to move the energies of the right channel over into the left, so balancing ourselves before we start. We can also use warmer water in the footsoak, and even just saying the affirmation '*I am not this body or mind, I am the spirit*' if we feel ourselves nodding off.

If we can be strong in our resolve in this way, then our body quickly learns who's the master and will respond properly in the future. This in turn will prove to be a great step forward in our progress, as for the first time our spirit will be asserting its needs over and above those of our ego.

HOW LONG SHOULD WE MEDITATE FOR?

This is a common question among those who are just starting out, and for obvious reasons. The conventional answer is 'as long as it takes', but in reality people usually suggest that newcomers meditate for around 10 minutes for each session. There really are no hard and fast rules, and while some newcomers find 10 minutes to be adequate, others prefer 20 minute sessions, or even 30 or 40. The thing is to go with what feels comfortable, and try to make sure that it fits in with your daily routine so that you can practice regularly.

Some people, particularly 'achiever types', try to approach Sahaj meditation as they would any other endeavour, and literally force themselves to sit for long periods to really 'give it a go'. This is counter-productive. There is no need to push things, and in fact the more we strain the harder it becomes. It is simply impossible to treat yoga meditation like a sport or exam subject. We cannot 'win', 'pass' or even 'excel' by working at it harder and longer, because true yoga only occurs when we let go of our egotistical urges and replace them with spiritual peace.

The Lord Buddha spent years struggling to achieve his spiritual enlightenment through fasting, penance and other austerities, but it was only when he was forced to stop through exhaustion that he attained Nirvana. In the end it is our Kundalini and not the rampant demands of our ego that will guide us and give us the time we need to meditate. We should of course still be diligent and maintain a regular daily meditation practice, but this should be done with a balanced sense of determination rather than a fanatical streak.

In the early days we may not be able to cope with more than 10 to 15 minutes at a time before our ego kicks in and we start worrying about missing trains, meals or that great movie on TV. We should, however, try and allow the Kundalini a respectable amount of time in which to perform Her tasks. This can take more

109

time when we are particularly under pressure, so we must be patient. Imagine that we only allowed our doctor one minute to examine us and prescribe? It would make the task rather difficult, wouldn't it?

It's much better to avoid being 'clock driven', and in fact we should try and get to a point where we can meditate without a clock or watch in the room, confident that we will spend the optimum time meditating and still not miss the bus! This may take some time to master, but it can be very satisfying to find that we are no longer ruled by unruly thoughts of minutes and seconds. The lucky ones quickly begin to enjoy their meditations so much that time flies by, and they are usually the ones who set aside extra time for unexpectedly longer sessions. They will set the alarm a little earlier in the morning, or perhaps start their evening session a little earlier too.

A good rule of thumb is that we should rise from our meditation having experienced at least a few moments of the 'silent stillness' that marks a true state of yoga. If the meditation is composed of frenetic thoughts from start to finish, we can probably assume that we need to cool down our right side, examine the state of our liver and perhaps spend a little more time clearing ourselves the next time around.

Most people find that a 20 minute meditation is optimum for the early days, perhaps rising to 40 or 50 minutes per session after a while, but this will definitely vary from person to person. However as mentioned before, it is infinitely better to complete two short 10 minute sessions every day, than miss a session each day and go for a 2 hour 'burn' at the end of the week to make up. There is little or no benefit in that, as gradually you will start missing out more and more sessions until you give up completely.

Can a short meditation ever be of value? Absolutely. Grabbing a quick moment to meditate in an emergency or when we are away from our home environment is an essential part of any yogi's spiritual arsenal. Never dismiss the power of a quick 5 minute session with our Kundalini raised and our attention at the top of the head. It can do absolute wonders to bring us back into a state of balance, to settle things down and restore calm. Use it often and everywhere. On the train, bus, park bench, even in the office restrooms when the going gets particularly rough.

Our meditation is our pathway to freedom, but in another sense it is also one of the most powerful and effective weapons in our personal armoury. Many's the time that a potentially fraught situation has been brought under control by a yogi simply putting their attention onto their Kundalini and to the top of their head, even while standing in front of a would-be protagonist! We have the power to alter the whole environment around us if we can take ourselves into any kind of thoughtless state - it's a fact. Because by doing so, we are surrendering the situation or problem to the Divine, and such genuine requests are never ignored.

We shouldn't be afraid to use these benevolent powers whenever they are needed. They don't expire, become exhausted or limit themselves in any way. As long as we remain connected through our meditation, we remain absolute masters of our universe. The only thing we have to do is realise it!

WHAT ARE WE AIMING FOR DURING MEDITATION?
We have already seen that the goal of any true yoga adept is to achieve the liberation of total self-knowledge. But of course that's easier said than done, especially when we are trying to juggle a busy lifestyle, job, relationships and family in the modern world. This is why it's best to take it one step at a time, focussing on each particular milestone on the journey, rather than worrying fruitlessly about our final destination.

The first target for successful progress in meditation is to achieve some sort of thoughtless awareness. We've talked about it as a form of stillness or peace, but in reality it is far more profound than that. Real thoughtlessness is to be found only when we have moved

111

above the thoughts of the mind, and have transferred the focus of our attention to the Sahasrara Chakra and beyond.

This is why practitioners often talk about 'taking the attention to Sahasrara' when guiding public meditations or in conversation about spiritual matters. This literally means moving the focus of our mind above the head to slow down the flow of thoughts.

In the early days it can be very confusing to understand how we can move our attention. Surely we can only do that by looking at something with our eyes, and if our eyes are closed, what are we using, our hearing? In fact our attention is very similar to our concentration, only without the hard work! The idea is not to intensely focus our mind on something, as if we are trying to make it move across a room, but to lightly allow our attention to drift to the top of our head, to the highest Chakra, and remain there no matter what.

Difficult as it sounds, over time we do become adept at moving our attention to the Sahasrara centre, and it is then that we start to experience the real meaning of thoughtlessness.

One of the most confusing parts of Sahaja Yoga for many people is this concept of taking the attention higher, especially if they have tried other forms of yoga or Buddhism which stress that they must be 'mindful' or use 'imagery' to help meditate. The point is that to traverse into a spiritual realm, one must really move beyond the senses and the cage of the mind. The Agnya Chakra which sits at the point of the 'third eye' in the forehead in this respect is really a false portal. Meditating on this centre offers an easy simulation of thoughtlessness, but it can not deliver real spiritual evolution because it is too closely connected with the ego, senses and material universe.

So how can we tell an Agnya meditation from the thoughtless kind? For one, if we experience any imagery, colours, patterns or bright white lights during our meditation, then we are probably

112

trapped at the level of the ego and the mind. This is a meditation which may have all the hallmarks of a real yoga, but in the long run it will take us nowhere, spiritually speaking. That's because this type of artificial meditation does not result in a connection between Sahasrara and Cosmos, and it is only through such a connection (as evidenced by the state of thoughtlessness or Nirvichara Samadhi) that we can achieve the spiritual growth we seek.

The state of thoughtlessness is also proof of the sublimation of our ego and super ego at the level of the Agnya, and so tells us that the powerful and nurturing energy of our Kundalini is reaching the Sahasrara Chakra in full force. This in turn indicates that our connection is growing stronger with each meditation and that we are being nourished by the flow of Vibrations that inevitably occur as a result of true yoga. Our state of thoughtlessness therefore becomes a sort of spiritual barometer which, along with Vibrations, lets us know how well we are progressing in our spiritual journey. Note that it doesn't tell us how far we've got, just how well we are doing.

It's important to stress that achieving the thoughtless state is not easy at all. We naturally think about things all the time, and it is just about impossible to stop this process of thinking. However what we are trying to do in meditation is slow the pattern of thoughts down to a less frenetic pace. When we are fairly new to meditation we should not expect to experience long periods of stillness at all, but should be grateful for whatever short periods we can achieve. These fleeting moments of calm may literally be seconds in length, but they build up over time to give us the yoga that we need. We just have to be patient and realise that as long as we persevere, we will eventually start to feel the kind of profound peace that comes from a truly satisfying meditation.

We can help ourselves achieve a deeper form of thoughtlessness by using a few techniques that have been passed down over time. For one thing we can make use of the element of fire to help open the Agnya and slow our thinking. By looking at a candle flame for a

113

few moments at the beginning of our meditation we help the Agnya clear, which in turn allows the Kundalini to pass through more freely to the Sahasrara at the top of the head. We don't have to spend long doing this, a minute or two is sufficient, and if we feel the thoughts starting to return after we close our eyes we can try gazing at the candle again for a moment or two.

We can also use mantras. We've already learned that the power of forgiveness is a very good way to help cleanse the Agnya, and indeed simply saying silently to ourselves, '*I forgive*', several times in the early part of the meditation is very effective in helping us go beyond the Agnya. Doing this releases subtle tensions that we may not even realise we have, and which may be holding us back from experiencing the peace of the meditation.

Another mantra which is commonly used at this stage is the Sanskrit word '*Neti*', which literally means '*Not this*'. By saying this mantra silently to ourselves we are distancing ourselves from the world of name and form, and thereby pushing ourselves more firmly into the meditative spiritual realm. After saying *Neti* sincerely and from the heart a few times, we may notice that our head has become lighter and that we are experiencing a deeper sense of calm inside and out.

None of these mantras should be used in a repetitive or automatic way, because this removes the power of the words to resonate with our subtle system. The rhythmic, repetitive, ritualistic chanting of mantras will only succeed in taking us into a trance like or self-hypnotic state, which again is of absolutely no benefit in spiritual terms. Meditation is neither trance, hallucinogenic rapture or self hypnotic illusion. It is a gentle and natural transition into a state of spiritually sublime peace and self awareness.

There are other more extensive Sanskrit mantras which we can use which are freely available as part of any public course in Sahaja Yoga meditation at your local meeting. Ask there for more details.

114

Be disciplined

As with everything we do, the more that we put into our yoga practice, the more we will get out. There are no short cuts to our evolution, although you wouldn't think so from reading some of the modern books on the subject. Our best friend is our diligence, and we need to remember that the journey is just as important as the destination.

For some people the hard part of their practice comes after they have been meditating for a year or two and they start to slip into a comfortable routine. We generally tend to gravitate towards comfort of all types, and try to avoid anything which is likely to be hard work. But of course in yoga we only grow though our efforts to overcome challenges.

We may have become comfortable with our yoga routine and even confident about our level of knowledge and expertise. In some cases we may even believe that we have overcome our problems and are on the final stretch of the journey, and maybe we begin to relax a little. After all missing a meditation here and there can't hurt can it?

The danger signs are when we start making excuses to ourselves, excuses that we know deep down are on shaky ground. We tell ourselves that we can miss meditations because we have reached a higher state or don't need them as much. Sometimes we may be tempted to group together with others who share our views, perhaps to share this weakening of resolve and so feel better. If we're all doing the same things and thinking the same, then surely we're all correct and the others are wrong?

We do ourselves a disservice by drifting in this way. The spirit recognises and responds to our desire, and if our desire is decreasing so much that we have to make excuses to ourselves, then we are cheating our own being, and our evolution will inevitably suffer.

This is not something that we should become guilty about either, we simply have to make a decision either to continue down the slope or take action to stop the rot. Missing meditations may be easy, but it is a very slippery slope. We may start by missing one a week, then two out of six, then every other evening meditation and suddenly we may find that we cannot experience the vibrations or the joy any more.

This in turn makes it harder to commit to the meditation practice and so the vicious circle starts to be formed. The reality of the matter is that slipping in our practice is a little like not brushing our teeth. For a while nothing appears to be wrong, then after a day or so we notice that our breath and mouth are not so fresh. Then we may start getting the occasional mouth ulcer or sore. Eventually of course, our gums attract disease and our teeth can begin to rot and fall out. By this time, of course, it's difficult and painful to take any corrective action, or even slow the rate of decline.

In the same way, if we allow our practice to slip we will probably not notice anything for a while, but then we will realise that it is becoming harder and harder to make the time to meditate. And when we do, the results are not as good as they were before. We may start to question our practice too, and start asking questions about the value of our journey and search for the truth in general.

Unlike tooth decay, however, we can restore our spiritual vigour simply by focussing our entire attention once more on our ascent. If we have a sincere desire to return to our evolutionary journey, and begin to meditate regularly again, we will slowly move back into balance and our peace will return. It needs determination, though, and not just a half-hearted attempt to stem the tide of negativity.

The disciplined practitioner who meditates every day without fail experiences improvement and growth in every aspect of their being. Any stress in their life disappears, and they start to enjoy the little things with total freedom. Most importantly, once their spiritual connection has been strengthened, they genuinely start to take control of their own destiny. It is not about experiencing miracles or profound experiences at the top of sacred mountains, but rather a deepening sense of self, an understanding of God and our overall relationship with the Universe, and an ability to see Divine work in every aspect of our lives. We literally experience a continual and glorious two-way flow of communication between our mundane material world and the spiritual universe.

To have discipline means to continue meditating even if we feel ill, tired, emotionally shocked or drained or under intolerable stress. It means that we don't give up even when we experience bad meditations which seem to be a waste of time. They aren't. It means that we don't listen to small voices of negativity, we listen to our heart and trust in ourselves to make the right choices for our long term benevolence. Above all to have discipline in our yoga means that we never give up, no matter how tough the internal or external battle becomes. We become true warriors of the spirit.

It is not necessary to become monk-like or ascetic, nor do we have to give up everything that we enjoy. That is not spiritual discipline, and those who believe that this is the only way to the spirit are mistaken. Instead our focus should be on transcending the mundane desires of material things through a natural process of meditative introspection. We learn what's good for us and what is not. We also learn the discipline that makes us strong enough to enjoy the fruits of the material world without guilt and without attachment.

Be patient
We want it now, and we don't want to wait. Why should we, when we have been taught from infancy that 'he who hesitates is lost?' We know that we have to go out and fight for what we want and that if we don't, someone else will. If we snooze, we lose. Everything in the modern world is geared towards speed and instant gratification; the 5 minute car wash, 3 minute meals, 1 minute laundry, 20 second ATM banking, 2 minute theatre. We're saving

so much time every day that it's a wonder we don't end up with a big fat surplus of minutes every twenty four hours.

But of course we don't. Because for some reason, all the time saving in the world still leaves us short. There are never enough hours in a day to get everything done, so it's hardly surprising that we don't want to wait for anything. And then along comes Sahaja Yoga and tells us that we need to be patient, and not expect that we will achieve huge and important changes in our life straight away. How frustrating is that?

The point is that nature and natural phenomenon do not operate on an urban speed, micro-minute, no-wait timetable. Nature takes her time to create and destroy, and we should take our cue from her gentle power and understand that anything pure and truthful will take time to flower. We don't expect a rose to grow and bloom in four hours, so why would we expect our spiritual evolution to work out completely in just seven weeks?

Of course there will still be milestones along the way which we can use to monitor our progress. It's just that we have to understand that patience is a key requirement for any spiritual practice. We need to be patient with ourselves and not expect too much, too early. We need to be patient with others when they do things which we consider silly or unnecessary. We need to be patient when our meditations are not going the way we want, and we feel frustrated and alone.

Above all, we need patience in order to savour and enjoy the deep sense of peace that comes from our yoga after we have been practicing for a while. One of the reasons why so many people fail to achieve anything through their yoga is that they get impatient when their progress doesn't match the speed of the rest of their lives. Why shouldn't they feel peaceful and joyful if they have diligently meditated twice a day for all this time? When they've followed all the instructions to the letter, footsoaking, balancing, clearing, mantras, candle treatments, attended classes regularly and done everything else they've been asked? There's clearly something wrong with the yoga in that case, because obviously they have done everything that's required and it hasn't worked.

In fact there are a huge number of factors which combine to determine the rate and depth of our experience in yoga, and time is a very minor one. The first is how much baggage have we brought with us to the table? If we come from a tortuous and hard bitten lifestyle, then it can be much harder for the Kundalini to cleanse the Chakra system and nourish the subtle energy flows. We may be situated in completely the wrong environment for spiritual growth, which in turn has to be sorted out so that we can start to ascend properly.

Our relationships, past karmas and character can also have a profound effect on our evolution. We all have some subtle damage of one sort or another, no person has a completely clean spiritual energy system, and the variations between the extent and type of the problems can be huge. Some people are so closed hearted or egotistical that the process struggles to work at all, and they may well need a long period of healing before they can expect to experience any regular profound moments in their yoga. This is not to say that they won't experience anything wonderful, it's just that it may take a little more time.

Even those who come to Sahaja Yoga from a supposedly spiritual background can have problems, as sometimes a little knowledge can be a dangerous thing. We think we know the answers when in fact we can barely frame the questions properly. The wise man tells us that in order to achieve true self knowledge, first we must empty our cup of previous ideas and conditionings in order to fill it again with the truth. Which can make it very difficult for those who have spent a lifetime seeking the truth and who have built up a huge storehouse of information and knowledge as they go.

The truly humble human being has the patience of a saint (and what an apt phrase that is!). They do not seek to rush the natural evolutionary process, but instead focus on enjoying the journey as it occurs, with all its ups and downs, surprises and shocks. This patience leads directly to the surrender of our selfish will to that of our Divine benevolence, which is essential if we are to cross the barrier of our ego. They also do not spend their time peering into the distant future to try and get a glimpse of the destination, because they realise that the real joy is to be found in the tiniest things happening right at this very moment.

Patience is a virtue, impatience a vice.

Be subtle
Obtaining self-realisation is a truly crucial point in anyone's existence. It gives meaning to our lives, it points us in the right spiritual direction and above all it gives us an unimpeachable connection to the subtle universe in which we exist. This Cosmos is not one that the scientists can perceive with a telescope, and it is considered by many people to be completely unreal. But whatever the rationalists think doesn't matter. The subtle universe exists, with them or without them.

However in some ways it too is an illusion of sorts. The spiritual universe exists only insofar as we can connect to it, and have a desire to perceive its workings. We can think of the complete universe as encompassing our individual spiritual energies, the channels that carry them, the Chakras, the Divine consciousness and associated collection of Deities, and spiritual entities and forces that we cannot see but which have a direct effect on our day to day existence.

This universe has been written about for thousands of years, and has been depicted in just about every religious text in existence. However most people in the modern world treat it as no more than a myth, something that has been created to scare the children. We have lost our sense of innocent wonder, our knowledge of God and our open minded and open hearted acceptance of the truth, no matter how strange it may appear. The modern world has instead come to believe that science and technology are the only roads to true knowledge. It is an unfortunate state of affairs in every way.

The spiritually adept, however, are indeed sensitive to the hidden Cosmos, and Sahaja Yogis use it specifically to evolve. The subtle universe exists in order to give form to the formless, to help human beings retrace their steps to their spiritual roots and return to their Creator, in line with their destiny. Because of this we should be aware that the subtle universe has many different layers and aspects. It exists, no question, but because it is described in a particular way does not mean that we can perceive every single aspect of it.

We talk, for example, of the Kundalini as rising through the centre of the spinal cord on it's way to the top of the head, and yet the actual path is in another dimension completely, deep in the heart of our subtle system. The use of the spinal cord as a reference point is merely a useful visual clue to help us fix our attention on the path so that we can encourage the process with our spiritual desire. However, even so, many people have reported that they can actually see the Kundalini pulsating as she moves up the central channel, which clearly shows that the subtle and physical dimensions are inextricably linked at every level.

If we lock ourselves too rigidly into the ritual of our yoga, we risk losing sight of a really important fact, which is that the work is always done by our attention, or more correctly, by the pure desire of our attention. When we say a mantra, or work on a Chakra with our hands, or raise the Kundalini with our fingers, we are simply providing a physical manifestation of the work of our spiritual attention, in order to make it easier to focus on the job in hand. Without the pure desire of our attention, we can never make our yoga work, no matter how much effort we put into doing the right things.

People often ask, for example, why physical techniques such as placing an ice pack on the liver or having a foot-soak are considered so important in Sahaja Yoga. The answer is that these actions give effect to our spiritual desire. When we make the effort to gather some ice and apply it to the region of our liver, we are of course physically cooling down the area around the liver, but more importantly we are asking the spiritual vibrational energy, in a subtle way, to cool down our right side and help us return to a state of balance.

In an ideal world, we could achieve this simply by sitting in meditation with our attention fixed at the Sahasrara Chakra, but this is an incredibly difficult thing to accomplish unless we are totally adept at our yoga. Many people find it almost impossible to focus on the formless or do subtle activities without some sort of logical physical action on which to put their attention, and which crucially can be repeated as needed.

The subtle universe is constantly at our disposal, even if we are not 100% convinced that it's there. Most of the time we cannot perceive any of it apart from the gentle play of vibrations, all we can experience are the results of our requests and prayers. We see that our liver gets cool when we apply an ice pack, which in turn removes agitation and brings a peaceful, balanced meditation. We don't know exactly how it works, but we experience the effects directly.

And herein lies the fundamental difference between authentic spiritual practice and the scientific world. The scientific world demands that hypotheses be proved, and that events be observable and predictable. The subtle universe, however, does not play by the rules of the senses, but instead works directly through the power of God. We know that it is there because we communicate with it and through it every single day, even if we cannot physically see or touch it. It is a gulf that is not easily bridged, and so science calls this subtle knowledge 'new age nonsense', while the spiritually adept deride science for being rigid, ineffectual and holistically ignorant.

In fact we can, and should, use the spiritual Cosmos as often as possible in our day to day lives to help our evolution. The more we

122

put our attention onto the subtle aspects of life, the stronger and more skilled we become. Even by talking about it with friends and strangers, we are strengthening our attention and gaining a better understanding of the power of God to transform our lives.

Unfortunately some newcomers find this focus on the subtle universe to be very challenging. It's not easy having been brought up in a secular, scientific world for many people to accept that there is another vital component of life and humanity, one which can be tapped into on demand. People simply do not believe that these unfamiliar subtle techniques work, and after a while the sheer embarrassment of trying to accept it can put people off and they drift away from the practice.

Those who remain, however, often do so because they begin to experience things that they never thought possible. Real joy returns to their lives, as they start to notice the significance in everything around them, and as they begin to experience the wonder of a life full of miracles. The first few events are usually put down to coincidence, but eventually they come to realise that there really is an unseen, benevolent agency which is in communication with us every second of the day.

It's a fabulously liberating experience because, perhaps for the first time ever, we realise that we are really not alone. That we can genuinely hold a real conversation with God and know that we are being heard, and that our purest desires are being acted upon for our ultimate benevolence. It changes everything.

Suddenly we notice that the world is chock full of significance. We see the hand of God everywhere, sending messages, arranging events, rewarding faith and love. It's as though a giant light bulb has been switched on, illuminating everything in a beautiful Divine glow. We learn to watch out for the signs, for the conversation, and to respond to it. It becomes our path to surrender and the eventual dissolution of ego.

Instead of being disappointed with our lives we actually begin to appreciate the lessons of life – 'how can I improve from this experience?' We recognise Divine love for what it is, a reflection of our own state of subtle being, a mirror which shows us just how open hearted and giving we are. Above all, we learn that the subtle universe has no other function than to help us fulfil our destiny, to give us divine guidance 24 hours a day, 365 days a year as and when we need it.

It's a magnificent feeling to be able to hold the hand of God as we clamber over the sharp stone shards which are scattered along the route to spiritual enlightenment.

Introspect

One of the hardest things that any person can do is examine themselves with a detached attitude, to identify weaknesses and strengths. We are simply not equipped to be totally objective, which makes it almost impossible for us to understand what we need to do in order to improve ourselves. But if we are serious about our spiritual journey, this is something that has to be done, and done properly.

Thankfully the journey comes with its own set of tools which give us the power to be constructively, rather than destructively, self critical. Once we have our self-realisation and have established our yoga through meditation, we can take advantage of our new enlightened attention to do a lot of the work. This attention becomes more and more detached as we progress, which in turn gives us the power to take decisions without focussing on a particular outcome.

If we need to change our environment or current relationships significantly in order to improve our rate of spiritual ascent, the enlightened attention allows us to see the whole picture rather than just a small part, so that we can understand why it is important and how it will benefit us in the long run. This in itself is a wonderful power to possess and one which can save us from hours of heartache and headache in our decision making process.

We also cleanse the Chakras which govern our use of wisdom in everyday matters. The wisdom we gain from this process of introspection and subtle cleansing puts things into perspective, and instead of looking for short term or material gain, we make decisions which are important for our long term spiritual ascent. Our newfound powers of discretion, the courage of the Heart, the innate innocence and wisdom of the Mooladhara Chakra, all combine to show us the optimum path to take in our new spiritual life.

At first it can be quite hard to relax and allow this process to happen without trying to interfere. Our ego tends to think that it knows best, and we can also easily find ourselves swayed by our emotional attachment to things, people or situations. In these cases the answer to our problem is often obscured behind a cloud of doubts, mind games and illusion. Everyone is familiar with those instances where we need to decide between two seemingly equal and beneficial options – it's torture as long as we vacillate between the two arguments.

The enlightened attention and innate wisdom of the yogi makes the decision process easier and more direct. We may still consider the options, but in the end we will feel the answer on our Chakras, through the vibrations we feel on our body (cool for yes, warm for no) and deep in our soul. The real problem in the early days often comes from the fact that we are reluctant to surrender to the obvious truth. We ignore the signals that we receive from our whole being, and instead tend to focus on the wearisome and spurious counter arguments generated by our ego.

But after we have been meditating for some time, we learn to recognise the signs much quicker, and become more willing to trust the subtle signals no matter what we may 'think'. This is when we truly begin to gain an insight into the ancient concept of 'Divine surrender' in its purest form.

We learn to trust the Divine power to guide us in all things, not as a slave, but as a willing and much loved disciple. We learn that if we need to overcome our natural right sided tendencies in order that we can move on in our spiritual journey, then we have to attend to it diligently and without making excuses.

We also learn to recognise the signs that tell us we should let go and move on, if we have become too attached to something or someone and it's slowing our spiritual evolution. We learn that things are not always as they seem, and that sometimes our mind and ego really do play tricks on us, and blind us to the truth.

We learn too, that there are some things deep within us that we try to avoid at all costs because facing them is just so painful, and we come to terms with the fact that we must deal with them if we are ever to improve. And so we allow ourselves to be gently guided towards the dark corners of our soul again and again, until finally one day we realise that we have finally passed the test and are no longer carrying that particular piece of baggage with us on the journey. And it feels like we've literally dropped a ton weight off our back.

And finally we come to understand that there is nothing that we cannot cleanse, clear or remove from our being if we have the will and strength of desire. We have the ultimate power of the universe at our disposal and nothing can stand in its way; it is our servant every bit as much as we are the servant of our spiritual destiny.

– CHAPTER FIVE –

Does one scent appeal more than another?
Do you prefer this flavour or that feeling?
Is your practice sacred and your work profane?
Then your mind is separated from itself, from oneness, from The Tao.
Keep your mind free of divisions and distinctions.
When your mind is detached, simple, quiet, then all things can exist in harmony,
And you can begin to perceive the subtle Truth.
Lao Tsu, The Hua Hu Ching

THE BENEFITS OF MEDITATION

One of the difficulties that many people face when they first start to meditate is working out whether they are doing the meditation properly and whether it is having a beneficial effect. Strangely enough this is often not so much of an issue in the first two weeks or so as it is later on, after the initial period of familiarisation is over.

The early days of meditation are usually marked by a general feeling of well-being. For many people, this is the first time that they will have experienced a true spiritual practice in action, and their subtle system really flowers under the attention. They feel happy, may start sleeping better and may find their heart opening in the most unexpected ways. For some the experience can be incredibly intense, with tears of release or feelings of overwhelming joy.

No two people are alike and so it is impossible to state how each individual reacts, but suffice to say it can be wonderfully elevating, confusing, exhilarating and scary all rolled into one kaleidoscopic mishmash. Or it can be very low key.

Whatever the response from the early process of self-realisation and meditation, pretty soon things start to settle down and life returns to what we think of as our 'normal routine'. Of course normal is a very subjective word, but in general the excitement can reduce considerably after the exhilaration of the first weeks or months, and this is when things start to become a little harder to gauge. It is at this point that some people give up or start to lose interest in the meditation, which is a shame because this is precisely when we have the most to gain by continuing.

In fact, during this next phase we start to engage in a very subtle battle between the head and the heart, or we can say the ego and the spirit. Up until the moment we gain our self-realisation we will have been under the complete 'control' of our ego; we have made decisions based on our desires and wants, we have experienced emotional crests and troughs, we have suppressed our true selves beneath an unconscious set of accumulated baggage which has ruled our lives.

How many of us have ignored the warning signs of a perilously rocky relationship which was clearly not good for us, but which filled some other need – usually fear or loneliness? How many have accepted situations which we truly did not enjoy, want or need, simply to maintain our popularity or status with friends and family? Who hasn't acted impetuously and stupidly and not regretted it afterwards? These are all signs of a perfectly normal lifestyle, but one that has been governed by the ego and superego in us. A life of compromise governed by our weaknesses. Even when we thought we were acting from the heart!

Now suddenly, after self-realisation, we recognise the spirit inside ourselves for what it is, our true guide. The ego suddenly has to operate alongside our enlightened spiritual attention, and so no longer maintains sole control of our actions and thoughts. For many of us, this fundamental spiritual shift is a traumatic change which doesn't sit well with our mental view of who we are. We may not realise it, but our ego finds it difficult to let go. It is a conditioned response, driven by a lifetime of its influence; wanting, planning, thinking and taking action. Suddenly it is sidelined.

The result of this inner turbulence can be that we find ourselves questioning our yoga, especially once the initial euphoria of spiritual release has subsided. Our ego is in effect asking 'Why do I need to meditate?' Our ego is trying to lead us back to our so called 'comfortable' life, baggage and all, where we can avoid the difficult challenge of facing ourselves in the quest for self knowledge.

There is no reason that this tussle between the heart and mind should stop us meditating or continuing on our spiritual journey. We must simply be diligent and refuse to be sidetracked into wasting time questioning our new experience. If we end up analysing everything surrounding our meditation then our mind has won, and we are taking ourselves away from the yoga. If we can simply learn to enjoy the experience without too many questions, then we can surrender to our spirit and start to really gain the benefit.

This doesn't mean at all that we should stop asking questions altogether when we start meditating. It's only human to be curious, especially if this is the first time that we have ever experienced a spiritual practice of this sort. However, the best type of enquiry is that which comes from the heart, with a positive outlook and which is designed to help us learn how to grow. If we spend our time on destructive thoughts, worrying why this is done this way, or things aren't done that way, then we miss out on fully enjoying the experience itself.

We may miss the joy which comes from a deep meditation in the evening, because we are too conditioned to accept that footsoaking actually works. We may miss the clues which the vibrations give us because we are too busy testing to see if they're real or just a result of self delusion. We can even mistake the whole purpose of yoga – to grow into a fully self-aware spiritual being – because we worry too much about the organisation involved in holding the meetings each week.

There are, however, some quite clear signposts which we can use to recognise that we are on the right path. These clues can be great pointers to our growing spiritual sensitivity, and a gauge as to how well we are progressing. Not every person will experience them with the same intensity, so we shouldn't try to 'tick the boxes' to show our progress. We can just try and keep an eye out for any of these things as we go along, and see whether we recognise any aspect in our relationships, our environment or life in general.

PEACE

We all seek peace in one form or another. Some look for it through nature's beauty, others take refuge in music or the arts. Some dedicate their lives to the search for inner peace through retreats, austerity and contemplation. One thing that is clear, however, is that real peace comes only from within. We can try and trigger this feeling through artificial stimulus or by choosing our environment with care, but in the end, if there is no peace inside, nothing can work to make it happen for us.

The truth is that peace is a combination of several factors, which separately play different roles in our lives, but when mixed together form a blanket of serenity which rejuvenates, invigorates and calms. In the first place, we need to surrender to the moment. This means that we must focus on every split second of our time without worrying about the future or the past. In addition we need to lose our expectations, we should demand nothing and enjoy everything. Finally we must learn how to be totally content, without guilt, fear or desire. These are easy things to write, but are clearly extremely difficult to achieve, which is where our yoga meditation comes into play.

Our first experience of the peace of a Sahaj meditation comes during the early days, when our spirit finds release in the touch of the Kundalini. Our mind, so used to working at a frantic pace, is

130

suddenly given time to quieten itself. The result is that we feel fabulous, and really start to appreciate things around us that we may have missed before.

Once the early days have gone, however, the mind once again feels impelled to return to its previous state, and it is at this point that we must really dig deep and focus on the beneficial effect of the meditation on our lives. If we look hard enough, we will notice that despite the fact that the 'everyday world' is returning to fill our attention once more, it has a different quality. We begin to experience the world through different eyes and with a wonderfully peaceful form of detached intelligence. This is one of the earliest signs that our meditation is starting to make subtle changes to our perception.

This detached viewpoint is really the precursor to the tranquil state that we seek from our meditations. We aim to become grounded, patient and gentle, and we look for our practice to give us a sense of peace that lingers long after we have finished our morning and evening meditations. Eventually we will be able to maintain this serene state at all times. We will actually have become the meditation; genuinely calm personalities, and not just on the outside.

One of the first signs that we are achieving our goal is when we begin to lose our irritability or tendency to flare into outbursts of anger. Things that before may have sent us off into a tirade, now merely amuse us. This is nothing more than a flowering of our increased sense of perspective. We learn what is really important in our world, and re-order our priorities to match. This increased self knowledge in turn helps us to become more detached about worldly matters that would cause panic beforehand. Money worries, career choices, relationships all take their proper place in our attention, instead of causing us to worry and lose sleep.

That's not to say that we stop worrying completely, there will always be things which affect and disturb us deeply, but our growing sense of life's priorities now helps us to deal with them accordingly. Without fuss or drama.

The ultimate form of peace, of course, comes from a lack of worthless desire. We lose our desire to achieve outcomes which we consider important, but are in fact trivial or even harmful. We learn to surrender to the gentle benevolence of our spirit, to trust that it will 'all work out for the best'. This is enlightened surrender, a real understanding of the pattern of life, God and the spiritual dimension in all its glory.

One who has wisdom here, who is devoid of desire and passions, attains to deathlessness, to peace, and to the unchanging state of Nirvana. The Lord Buddha, Sutta Nipata 204

JOY

When most people think of joy, they link it with feeling happy. We associate the two together and consider them to be almost interchangeable. 'It was a very joyful occasion, and everyone was very happy.' To feel joy on its own, however, is not something that we commonly talk about. We generally don't say that it was a very joyful wedding, or that we felt joyful meeting an old friend. Perhaps because it is considered too old fashioned?

The fact is that few of us have a real idea of what joy is. We lump it together with other vague words such as bliss, and use it to indicate an almost mythical state of rapture. But joy has a reality, and a unique one at that. Like peace, joy has a complex and yet elegant set of components that make it what it is. And like peace, without any one of them, it disappears.

Joy is silence. It is the silence of absolute completeness. Joy is an absence of everything; emotion, desire, happiness, sadness, pain and ecstasy. We are really truly joyful only when we are complete in every way. Anything less is a pollution of that pure state. Even bliss, a much misused word as well, can be thought of as a destroyer of joy. For when we are blissful we experience something which

132

removes the silence of pure joy. Joy is infinitely deep, infinitely intangible and eternally sublime.

Our meditation gives us joy in the silence. At first these sublime moments are so tantalisingly brief that they are more frustrating than soothing. But soon we begin to experience a little more of the silence each meditation, and slowly we begin to perceive the faint outlines of the reality of joy. At the same time, we may experience joy outside of meditation, for example when we experience the raw beauty of nature and 'feel' it, rather than mentally manipulate it. For action is also a killer of joy. To sit in a summer meadow with no thoughts, no desires, totally complete in every cell is real joy. It demands nothing, and just is. We learn after a time that it is possible to be totally lost in joy through silence, and more importantly that this state is of itself complete. It is a marvel.

We may be able to recognise the onset of true joy in our lives when we feel a deep seated contentment with simple things which appear trivial. When we can feel as peaceful washing the dishes as listening to a sublime concert. When even the severest test leaves us with nothing more than a genuine gratitude for the lesson learned.

DETACHMENT

Detachment, when misunderstood, appears to be a very harsh word. It smacks of cold-heartedness and disdain. In the wrong context it speaks of uncaring selfishness and cruelty. But when it is experienced in its proper framework, we see it for what it truly is – a liberator. To be truly detached is to be free of the chains of emotion and mind. We can love unreservedly and without the need for a response. We can give our time, care and consideration to all, without favouring any one person or situation.

Some people find it hard to understand what detachment actually means, so perhaps an example will help. Imagine we are sitting in a cinema watching a very good film. We are engrossed in it, moved by it. We laugh and cry at the action as the plot progresses, and respond with deep emotions at critical times. However, despite our involvement, and even the very real tears that we may cry when provoked by the storyline, deep down in our being we know that it is 'just a film'. We know that soon it will be over and the play we are watching will give way to another reality outside the theatre. So too with life. As we develop our detachment, we start to watch the play of life as if viewing a great drama.

We are equally as involved in the plot, scenes and characters; moved to tears and laughter by events, but deep down we realise that life is really just a huge divine drama, played out for our enjoyment and benevolence. In this way we remain detached from all the highs and lows, keep a sense of proportion and yet stay completely involved in everything that is going on. It's a perfect balance between the spiritual reality and material experience, and once we achieve a deeply held sense of detachment, we learn how to really enjoy life. Joy becomes a reality.

Those who are detached in a loving way are a source of immense strength to everyone around them. People seek their advice, treat them as a wise guide and trust them completely. Detached wisdom speaks from the heart and from the spirit and so carries the weight of the universe as its truth. It may take some time to recognise the growing detachment inside ourselves once we start to meditate, but it comes nonetheless, slowly and surely, to all those who practice diligently.

We may find that we start to be more forthright and confident in our dealings with others. Which in turn makes us sought after as a source of wisdom in times of crisis. We find that our detachment means that we can always see the best for others, even when their problems appear to be insoluble. We begin to realise that our time is best used when it is freely offered to those who need it, and we begin to be less concerned about our own insignificant wants and needs.

Above all, our growing detachment shows up as a new and purer kind of love, unfettered by motive or design. We don't love because we have to, because it is expected of us or simply because we seek something in return. We begin to love because it gives joy. Because it showers the environment with vibrations and spirituality, and because it is the purest form of Divinity that exists. We love in the same way a baby loves, without agenda or manipulation.

On a subtle level detachment reflects our release from the five senses and from our conditioned characteristics. Pure unsullied detachment proves that we are freeing ourselves from the cage of our ego and superego, and that we have finally overcome our emotional dependencies. To be detached means that we have no real desires. We don't care whether we sleep in a bed or on the floor. We are unconcerned with the state of the weather or the quality of the food. We just enjoy everything.

For some people this sounds like dangerous fanaticism or even mindless insanity. They think that to be detached means that we give up our passion and our humanity and become soulless and dead. In fact true detachment is incredibly energising. It gives us a stability and a peace that smoothes our spiritual journey and awakens the full glory of our existence. If we can enjoy the really simple things in life, then our simple lifestyles become nothing less than a source of constant joy.

And as for being passionless? The detached person actually enjoys everything life has to offer in a truly profound way. For example, music comes alive because we pay no attention to the egotistical aspects of its production, but instead focus happily on the vibrational resonance it sets up in our heart and Chakras. Without a measure of detachment we might worry about whether it's appropriate to enjoy the piece, whether it is being played correctly, who the musicians are and so on. Detachment gives us simplicity, and simplicity gives pure, unsullied Divinity.

EMOTIONAL STABILITY
We live in a very volatile world, and are used to the 'ups and downs' of surviving in an environment that appears to be growing

more unpredictable as each day passes. We consider it normal to have to fight for a living and to put up with the disappointment and challenges of a hard life. Even the everyday cynicism that we regularly encounter nowadays is taken as an inextricably embedded part of the modern lifestyle. Many of us have adapted well enough to even 'thrive' in the cut and thrust of 21st century living, and consider it exhilarating and exciting. At least as long as we're young and things are going well. The less developed world looks on at our wealth, rampant consumption and social system and envies us our success.

However, in a thousand little ways, we do suffer for our modern dream life. We may learn to tolerate stress, and even to feed off it. We may learn to be comfortable with our suspicion of others and our fear of change and progress. We may even be happy with a life which runs through a constant, grinding, up and down cycle of good and bad, happy and sad, boom and bust. It's not perfect, but hey, just look at the perks!

Deep down, though, many of us realise that this is not a healthy way to live. Not just physically but emotionally. We understand that our existence is almost comical in its precariousness. That at any moment our death defying tightrope act can come crashing to the ground through no fault of our own, causing untold trauma to ourselves and our family. This is the ever present subconscious threat of the modern age, that we are not really in control of our destiny.

However the fact is that we can take control of our lives in more ways that we think. It may sound glib, but once we start to meditate and gain the first inklings of true self-knowledge, we begin to understand exactly how far from reality we have strayed in pursuit of the material dream. We begin to recognise again the important things in life and regain our perspective on what's important and what's not. Even this simple first step in self awareness is enough, believe it or not, to change the whole tenure of our life and give us the confidence to wrest back our dignity and purpose in ways we could never imagine.

So one of the first benefits of the meditation is that we start to become more stable in our emotional makeup. Instead of clinging desperately to our unpredictable, runaway rollercoaster of a life, we start to create some real order out of the chaos. For one thing, we don't react to the extent we did when faced with dramatic events in our lives. We find that we can cope with situations that previously would have had us reaching for medication, and more importantly, we begin to lose the constant underlying anxiety that may have been a part of our subconscious for as long as we can remember.

None of this happens overnight of course, and in the early days we're still susceptible to being knocked off balance by large shocks and events, but gradually over time we become grounded in a truly remarkable way. It's a great feeling to feel in charge of our destiny once again, and to laugh at things which in the past would have floored us completely.

This new found resilience and stability also has a profound effect on our personal relationships too, which are often the most precarious aspects of our existence. Much of the emotional turmoil from relationships comes from the fact that we often don't fully understand who we are, which in turn makes it difficult for us to relate to others properly. We may feel that we are in love, but do we really know what that means? And who exactly is the 'me' that's in love anyway? Is it this fun loving, carefree person or the serious, thoughtful and rather timid inner being? This confusion is a commonplace cause of many of the problems that we experience in our dealings with friends, family and loved ones.

Our yoga takes away the confusion of self. It may not be easy to face facts, but eventually we understand exactly who we are and what we want out of life, and we become comfortable with our strengths and weaknesses. That's not to say that we don't want to improve, because that's an integral part of any real spiritual journey, but we gain patience and a longer term view of the process as we go deeper.

PATIENCE

We are taught from an early age to expect instant gratification. And why not? We live in a microwave oven, fast burger, quick cash, instant lotto, live now kind of world. Where's the percentage in hanging around for others? You snooze, you lose! The problem, of course, is that this kind of lifestyle is unremittingly brutal and can never provide any real satisfaction. Nor do we seem to gain any extra time or leisure from being able to cook dinner for two in 3 minutes. In fact, the more instant our life becomes, the less free time we seem to have. Strange isn't it?

The reality is that it's hard to find time for ourselves when we're constantly running to keep up with a life crammed full of instant materialism. For instance, we don't just go on vacation, we have to DO, DO, DO everything possible while we're there, just to get our money's worth. And so we totally exhaust ourselves going on tours, shopping, diving, climbing, eating, dancing, drinking, socialising, sunbathing, photographing. Phew! It's exhausting just thinking about it.

This type of approach to life is a common part of many people's existence. It's as though we have to do everything we can today, just in case there really isn't a tomorrow. But really this running to stand still is all an illusion. Our busy lifestyle is by definition a shallow one, since there's no way that we can possibly fit all this activity into 24 hours and still have time to savour each experience properly. Something has to suffer and it's usually the details.

Ask most people what they did on holiday and they'll tell you about the great sights they saw, the grand events, the glamour, the extremes in weather, environment or people. But they'll be hard pressed to remember the small things, like the market they passed through on the way to the cathedral, or the beautiful flowers they

138

saw on the path to the beach house. Yet it is the small things which give substance to the reality of the whole experience.

Meditation teaches us to enjoy the journey as a whole and not to waste time peering into the future to catch a glimpse of the destination. We learn that the flowers at our feet are unbelievably fragrant and beautiful, if only we would stop for long enough to appreciate them. We realise that patience is a power that cannot be cherished too much. It is the bedrock of peace, contentment and our spiritual desires. 'All good things come to those who wait', is an ancient proverb, and how true it is.

All too often in our lives we feel impelled to rush around doing, achieving and succeeding, as though these are important milestones which define who and what we are. But the reality is that we are who we are, not what we achieve. And through meditation we discover a richness of the spirit which is beyond even the most vivid of our imaginings.

BALANCE

So what exactly is balance? We often hear someone described as a balanced person, and yet many of us have no clear idea of what this means. Are they good at tightrope walking? Do they have a natural gait when they run? Or is it simply an opposite to 'unbalanced'. We tend to understand the term unbalanced much better, don't we? Someone who is a little 'off the rails', neurotic maybe, prone to bouts of anger and emotional trauma.

So doesn't someone who is balanced exhibit the opposite of these traits? Well perhaps. But in spiritual terms, the idea of balance goes way beyond mere emotional makeup. This is because, in general emotional terms, being balanced and unbalanced tends to suggest an involuntary situation, it implies either a personality flaw or a blessing. Whereas in the spiritual dimension the attribute of balance is definitely something that can be acquired, polished and cherished over time. And conversely a lack of balance is something that can be removed from our lives completely, through diligence and patience.

So back to the original question. What exactly is balance, in a spiritual sense? Well on one level it denotes someone whose subtle energies flow freely around their spiritual system. They do not suffer from exhausted right or left channel problems, and consequently their Chakras are clear and open to the passage of the Kundalini up the central channel. These people maintain their balanced state through regular meditation and good living, and ensure that their lifestyle, attention and goals all focus on sustaining their spiritual evolution through stability.

Achieving this kind of equilibrium in our lives requires real determination, especially since we usually have to juggle the demands of our hectic day to day lifestyles with the need to maintain our spiritual focus. We do, however, experience this form of balance in a real sense when we touch that peaceful state in our meditation, and when we are placed in auspicious environments such as nature and artistic beauty. It is the calm at the end of a busy day, and the exhilaration at the end of a depressing one.

On another level the state of balance is quite simply the now. It is the total cessation of worries and desires, and the enjoyment of the present moment. The spiritually balanced person is a rock, neither ecstatic nor deflated, happy or sad. They do not seek entertainment or shun it, and they certainly do not know boredom. The balance they achieve through their meditation makes them completely secure in themselves and resistant to the ups and downs of life's surprises.

Eventually, after we have been meditating for a while, we notice that we become steadier in all aspects of our life. It is not that we become boring or dull, but rather that our experiences all start to become meaningful, no one more than another. Where before we might have sought out exciting events in our lives, suddenly we are content to enjoy the simple things.

We no longer need to be entertained, insofar as we learn to entertain ourselves from within. The sight of a beautiful flower, the sound of a church bell at noon on a dark blustery day, the splash of a dirty puddle. All are a part of God's beautiful play and can be enjoyed and relished as much, if not more, than a prestigious Philharmonic concert or a riveting Oscar winning movie.

Where once we may have been fearful of surprises, we now take them in our stride, as just one more event to experience in this glorious life of ours. Balance brings with it harmony, as we learn how easy it is to get along with our fellow human beings if we simply help them to help themselves. A balanced outlook also allows us to forgive, love and comfort without hesitation whenever and wherever necessary. We discover that it is the greatest pleasure in the world to unstintingly give of ourselves wherever and whenever.

True spiritual balance is the bedrock of peace and tranquillity, which in turn are the components we find at the heart of our yoga. So what is balance? It is our yoga, made manifest in our subtle spiritual system, in our Chakras, and in our emotional evolution. It is the causeway which leads to our eventual Moksha or liberation, the bridge across which we must pass in order to complete our evolutionary journey.

CREATIVITY

We live at a time when creativity is seen either as a passport to material riches, or as something to be cynically criticised and attacked. Those who can, create, but timorously and always with a guarded eye turned towards the criticism of others. Artists doubt the value of their work, until they either give up in despair, or – hiding behind an artificially pumped up ego –they manage to assert their mastery and gain recognition through sheer grit and dogged determination.

However as any true artist will readily admit, real creativity is much more than a super charged ego, a fancy car and some astute self-promotion. It is a secret, magical alliance between talented and heartfelt application and divine inspiration. This combination of heart and spirit is what gives sublime art its power to shape epochs.

141

We can usually recognise the divinity of true art just by measuring its enduring and widespread appeal.

All human beings have the capacity to use divine inspiration to produce beauty. The ability to create is not given solely to those who are talented, any more than the right to breathe goes only to those who are handsome. We need to rediscover our creative confidence, and most importantly learn how to create beauty from the depths of our heart, and this can only really be achieved if we unleash the power of the subtle spiritual energy inside ourselves to its fullest potential.

Once we start to clear out the Swadhishthan Chakra through meditation, we gain the ability and the courage to recognise where our creative talents lie. We may not be naturally gifted in any particular field, but we learn that even the most humble artistic effort is nothing more than an offering to God, delivered from the heart to the source. Those who may not have written a word are impelled to create rich and meaningful poetry, the tuneless learn to sing, the tongue tied become orators.

Most importantly of all, meditation gives us all the power to be creative in the way we make our choices in life. We learn to spread our wings and believe that we can fly to those far-off horizons which intimidated us before. We surrender our decisions and efforts to the great spiritual journey, and by so doing we free ourselves from the cage of fear we have erected around our lives. And we learn that creative experimentation is a talent to be treasured, not feared and locked away. For if we do not experience the world, how can we be said to be fully living in it?

So we should test ourselves as we progress in our meditation. Experiment with our creative urges, indulge in whatever artistry our spirit suggests, without fear or trepidation. We are our own creative master and our contribution to the world is valuable, unique and genuinely worthy of praise.

MENTAL AGILITY

We think too much, and yet paradoxically this over thinking does not necessarily result in better decisions. In fact, at its extremes, our hyper active mental processes actually impede our ability to function efficiently. Ironically enough, people nowadays are often praised for being 'great thinkers'. Even in olden times, great philosophers and poets were lauded for their ability to reason. But what these plaudits failed to acknowledge is the role of the spiritual dimension in all great works of these humanitarians.

Throughout the ages many great sages and philosophers have changed the shape of human society through their words, writings and spiritual insights. They, and many great artists also, have also freely admitted that their moments of inspiration were divinely triggered, with no conscious thought behind them.

'The glow of inspiration warms us; it is a holy rapture,' explained the Roman poet Ovid, born in 43 BC. His fellow countryman, the philosopher and statesman Cicero, concurred. *'There never was a great soul that did not have some divine inspiration'* he is quoted as saying.

Socrates too, some 300 years earlier, knew of the reality of this power. *'That showed me in an instant that not by wisdom do poets write poetry, but by a sort of genius and inspiration; they are like diviners or soothsayers who also say many fine things, but do not understand the meaning of them.'*

The greatest thinkers of our modern age have also instinctively understood how inspired thought occurs. *'The finest emotion of which we are capable is the mystic emotion. Herein lies the germ of all art and all true science. Anyone to whom this feeling is alien, who is no longer capable of wonderment and lives in a state of fear is a dead man.'* Albert Einstein (1879 –1955).

So if we realise that the power of truly wise thought comes not from the mind, but from the spirit of man, we can begin to understand just how crucial yoga is to our ability to 'think'. On one level the results of meditating mean that we are able to think clearly, without mental clutter or distraction. Instead of reacting to a situation by fruitlessly examining past events, irrelevancies and the unknown future ramifications, we can focus on dealing with the present, the impact on the now.

By naturally adopting this clear headed approach, problems can be solved in a fraction of the time it might normally take, and decisions can be made with confidence. Perhaps most importantly, we can also make out the wood for the trees; we can see everything in its right perspective and not be distracted by unimportant matters when we make our decision.

Beating fatigue

There are other tangible benefits which come from reducing our general rate of thinking through yoga meditation. For example, we regain the stamina which would otherwise be spent in worrying about situations, problems and events. It is a fact that many people in the modern world now exist in a constant state of 'tiredness'. One of the most frequent complaints at the doctor's surgery is that of 'fatigue', and the advice we are usually given is to 'get a little rest' or 'take some time off'. But are these really the best solutions? If we look carefully at the root cause of most of this fatigue, we'll see that it generally occurs in those who are suffering from stress in one form or another; stress caused by thinking and worrying too much which in turn makes them think and worry too much, to the point where they can't even get a good night's sleep. It's a vicious circle of the worst kind.

If we can therefore reduce the stress, we can remove the cause of the weariness, and we already know that meditation is the perfect way to reduce stress and restore our subtle system to a state of equilibrium. Stress overloads the right channel, which results in our excessive thinking. This usually shows up as a hot liver in Sahaja Yoga terms, and can easily be cured by adopting a sensible diet, meditating with a focus on cooling down the right side and by consciously trying to avoid situations which aggravate our thinking process.

The reason we become tired so easily when under these stressful situations is that the left channel is desperately trying to help cool down our over active right side, in order to restore some sort of balance to our subtle system. The left side energies start to move across to cool down the right, and as a result the left side becomes exhausted itself, at which point we start to feel tired. It's nothing more than a very sophisticated safety mechanism going into action. Under normal circumstances we would heed the subtle warning and slow down, sleep a little longer and take care of ourselves. The problem is that in the modern era we don't accept the need to slow down to avoid stress, there's too much pressure to keep going no matter what.

As a result we continue the assault on our right side, thus over exhausting both channels until eventually, unless we take drastic action, we collapse, either through mental or physical illness. The sad thing is that this problem can occur to any person, no matter what age, and often strikes the young at the very time when they should be enjoying their most productive years.

Don't worry, be happy
Our mental processes also benefit from meditation by becoming more agile. People generally operate in life through the natural interaction of their ego and superego. Whilst this can work fine in ordinary situations, it can cause problems in a crisis, when our conditionings and ego start to collide under duress. We all know people who have become almost paralysed by indecision where a decision is urgently needed in a serious matter. Once we start to meditate, we lose much of our unhealthy over reliance on ego and emotion, and can start to make decisions based on our instinctive and detached feel for a situation or event.

This may seem like a dangerous process, but only if we are afraid to surrender our lives to the guidance of our spiritual connection.

Yes it does need a leap of faith, and yes it is a hard thing to do, but if we can grow strong enough to make the adjustment, there is no question that the results can be astounding.

Not only will we be able to relax more easily and enjoy our lives more, but we will also start to understand that we are never really alone, no matter where we are or what we are doing. Our actions and the results of those actions are always subject to a divine guide. Of course things may not turn out exactly as we expected or wanted, and occasionally they may even appear to have gone completely awry, but if we continue to meditate in full confidence, things will always work out for our ultimate spiritual benevolence.

ATTENTION

We 21st century dwellers have very little concept of attention. We understand when someone talks about concentration or focus, but the idea of attention is alien to us. Which is a shame, because it is clear that many of the problems that afflict the modern age come from a general degeneration of attention.

Our attention is that part of us which channels our senses and conscious focus towards a point. When we look at a cup of tea, we can either simply gaze at it, with our mind wandering or we can focus on it and really examine the cup and the tea with our full concentration. The difference between concentrating our mind on something and putting our full attention on it, is that the latter means that we are using our whole subtle system as well as our mind and senses.

After we have received our self-realisation and are meditating regularly our attention becomes active. This means that when we put our attention onto something or someone, we are focusing our whole spiritual system and divine connection onto that target. We do not have to see someone physically with our eyes in order to place our attention on them, nor do we even have to know them or have met them. Our enlightened attention acts through the power of our yoga, and because of this it acts without needing our mental control.

All of Sahaja Yoga practice is done through the exercise of our subtle attention, which translates our inexact needs and desires into actions that will benefit us on our evolutionary journey. When we work on our Chakras and subtle system, it is our attention that is doing the real work, by desiring that our system is cleansed of impurities. It is not the fact that we say mantras or use the vibrations on our hands that does any of the subtle work. It helps to remember this when we practice yoga techniques which seem strangely physical like footsoaking, or the candle or ice pack treatments. It is not the physical action which does the subtle work, it is the full force of our dynamic enlightened attention desiring a spiritual result which makes it happen.

That is why it is important for us to remain thoughtless when we practice any Sahaj technique, such as meditation workshops or clearing the Chakras. If we start to think hard about what we are doing, our ego obstructs the pure work of our subtle attention and prevents the spiritual process from working properly. We literally get in the way of our own potential success.

However when we are thoughtless, with our attention firmly placed at the top of the head at the Sahasrara Chakra, then our spiritual connection is established, our yoga powers the flow of the vital energies, and our pure desires manifest for our benevolence.

Our attention is under constant attack from the clamour and distraction of the modern lifestyle. Our senses stagger under the assault to our eyes and ears which come from modern day media, advertising and entertainment. We swim through a constant avalanche of noise from billboards, radio, television, shop windows, magazines, newspapers and our general environment, all exhorting us to accept their propositions in one way or another.

These material world blandishments can eventually wear away our spiritual defences over time, which is why we feel so tired and drained when we have been exposed to a lot of this mental pollution. Meditating every day helps to restore our balance and centre our attention, so that we are once again in the heart of the spiritual peace. Once we have been meditating for a while we learn to recognise the signs of a fragmented attention – the restless feeling, the dissatisfaction, the agitation – and know to take rapid steps to correct the problem before it gets worse.

It is hardly surprising that we see more children suffering from attention problems at home and in school nowadays. They bear the brunt of many more attacks than any other part of society, and are pathetically ill-equipped to deal with the results. A fragmented attention also feeds back into our Agnya Chakra via our ego and fuels our thinking, which in turn takes us right back to the problems of stress and the right side. Small wonder, therefore, that so many people come away from long term exposure to the urban lifestyle drained and shell-shocked.

We need to nurture our attention with the kind of gentle love that helps it stay pure and strong. We learn through yoga how to channel our attention towards beauty and truth, rather than waste it on shallow, commercial rubbish. We start to use our attention in a positive way, to channel good throughout our environment and across the world. By doing this we also strengthen our yoga and enhance our overall spiritual growth.

Our attention is a precious part of our being. It is intrinsically linked with all aspects of our spiritual ascent and for that reason has to be treated with the utmost respect. We must learn to avoid abusing it, and where we feel there are problems we must take rapid steps to rectify the causes and return ourselves to a state of repose. If we can do this and maintain our subtle attention as it is meant to be, we will gain significant benefits in all aspects of our meditation, yoga and evolutionary journey.

Our attention should constantly be focussed on our spiritual ascent!

HEALTH

The human body is a miracle of biological engineering. With around 100 billion neurons in the brain, 40 million olfactory receptor cells to help us smell and around 130 million retinal receptor cell rods to let us see, this delicate but incredibly complex shell is much more than simply a bundle of skin and bone.

It is only relatively recently, however, that scientists and doctors have started to concede that there might be a real and definable connection – holistic, if you will - between the physical side of us and the invisible, but equally important spiritual body.

The body's nervous system is the instrument of consciousness, transmitting and translating the information gathered by our senses (hearing, touch, sight, taste and smell) to the brain for processing. Nerves are spread out across the body, but also form clusters known as plexuses. It is interesting to note that this nervous system, which controls the physical flow of signals to and from the brain, appears to have a direct correlation with our Chakras, which in turn affect not only the physical side of us, but also our emotional, mental and spiritual make up. The Chakras also have direct links with the immune, endocrine and lymphatic systems.

The Chakras correlate to the physical nervous and endocrine systems as follows:

Mooladhara	– Pelvic plexus: Excretory systems, genitals etc.
Swadhistan	– Aortic plexus: Lower abdomen, kidneys etc
Nabhi	– Solar plexus: Liver, stomach
Heart	– Cardiac plexus: Heart, lungs.
Vishuddhi	– Cervical plexus: Arms, neck, mouth, etc
Agnya	– Optic chiasmus: Pineal & pituitary bodies.
Sahasrara	– Limbic system

149

So we know for example that whilst the stomach gives us our physical sense of satisfaction after a good meal, it is the Nabhi Chakra which provides the ultimate spiritual satisfaction that comes with self-realisation and meditation. In the same way the lack of confidence which can stem from a weak centre Heart Chakra, may well be reflected in palpitations and other physical symptoms when we are afraid or nervous.

The effect of meditation on the physical body

The body's nervous system, which is part of an ultra sophisticated control mechanism, is divided into three main parts; the central, peripheral and autonomic nervous systems. These systems control how we act and perceive our universe through the senses, and the autonomic system also governs the automatic running of our bodies by controlling essential non-conscious tasks, such as the rate of our heart beat and constriction and dilation of the blood vessels.

One of the beneficial side effects of a peaceful and thoughtless meditation is that our autonomic system automatically keeps any unnaturally excessive physical activity in our body to a minimum. Since this system is also the part which governs the threat response mechanism within us all (which in the modern world can be damagingly over excited through constant stress) this serenity can prove to be of major benefit to our health. It has been suggested that this is accomplished through the improved energy flows which occur at the Limbic area (i.e. the Sahasrara Chakra at the top of the head) which is linked to the sympathetic nervous system.

In addition, Sahaja Yoga practitioners have been found to exhibit higher levels of endorphins than usual, which are known to activate the body's immune system. (*See Professor U.C.Rai, Medical Science Enlightened, 1993, L.E.T., p. 64*) This in turn is believed to increase the levels of antibodies which help fight against disease.

The liver and Sahaja Yoga.

The body depends on the liver to perform a large number of vital functions which can be divided into the following categories:

i) Cleansing blood:
* metabolising alcohol, drugs and chemicals
* neutralizing and destroying poisonous substances

ii) Regulating the supply of body fuel:
* producing, storing and supplying quick energy (glucose) to keep the mind alert and the body active
* producing, storing and exporting fat

iii) Manufacturing essential body proteins involved in:
* transporting substances in the blood
* clotting of blood
* providing resistance to infection

iv) Producing bile which eliminates toxic substances from the body and aids digestion.

v) Regulating our hormonal balance:
* sex hormones
* thyroid hormones
* cortisone and other adrenal hormones

vi) Regulating body cholesterol by producing it, excreting it, and converting it to other essential substances.

vii) Regulating the supply of essential vitamins and minerals such as iron and copper.

viii) Performing literally hundreds of other specific functions!

In fact just about everything that we swallow that is absorbed into the bloodstream ends up passing through this essential organ. As well as being the largest organ in the body it is also the only one which is capable of self regeneration. Whilst there is still much that is unknown about the full functionality of the liver it is probably fair to say that it is central to the body's metabolism, or the process by which living matter is produced, maintained or destroyed.

Ancient and modern.

Bearing in mind the obvious importance of this organ to our overall physical well being, it is no accident that the ancient practices of Indian Ayurvedic and Chinese medicine place a significant amount of focus on the liver. Its role in keeping the body free of harmful toxins and regulating our hormone levels means that it is clearly a vital link in the interaction of mind and body. This is why it's easy to directly trace its influence in things like the oscillating mood swings caused by fluctuations in our blood sugar levels or hormonal secretions, and its effect on our energy levels through the application of bile to our digestive system.

In one area, however, modern Western medicine deviates from ancient lore, and that's with respect to the significance of heat in the liver. Both Indian and Chinese medical practice acknowledge the effect of a 'hot' liver on the individual, and in fact offer specific remedies with which to 'cool' down this important organ. One such herb, for example, gardeniae jasminoidis (zhi zi) - otherwise known as the 'happiness herb' - is renowned for its effctiveness in removing the internal 'heat' which can cause irritability, restlessness and insomnia.

Sahaja Yoga also recognises this ancient wisdom and recommends that practitioners make an effort to keep their liver cool in order to improve their meditation and enhance their spiritual growth. The popular Sahaja Yoga Liver Diet is an example of the kind of useful treatment that can be used as necessary. The diet is really no more than a recommendation to eat sensibly to avoid degrading the important purifying functions of the liver. Details of the diet can be obtained from any international Sahaja Yoga centre.

Practical uses of Sahaja Yoga for health

In general our Sahaja Yoga meditations are a highly effective way of combating day to day ailments and resisting general health problems. We cannot become immune to illness, but we can use our meditation to make us hardier and more able to avoid the kind of medical problems which are considered the norm in today's hectic, stressful lifestyle.

There are also a number of practical steps we can take to improve this beneficial process, which also helps our Chakras and subtle system. These techniques are generally used both during and outside of our meditations, and are very effective in improving all aspects of our physical and spiritual well being.

★ Breathlessness and panic attacks.

Often these types of attack can be caused by an obstruction in the Heart Chakra. We can work on this centre at any time, whether in meditation or not, by breathing slowly and deeply in and out for a while with our right hand placed over the heart area. By doing this we channel vibrations and our loving attention to the centre to help it clear and open up more.

★ Neck pain.

This can be caused by an obstruction on the Vishuddhi Chakra. In this case we can place our right hand over the painful area during meditation or massage the area with oil, whilst reaffirming 'I am not guilty' 16 times. Guilt, which reflects a deep seated lack of self respect, is directly associated with this Chakra.

We can also help this Chakra stay clear and open by talking sweetly and avoiding arguments wherever possible. Harsh words have an immediately detrimental affect on this centre, and often we will start coughing or instantly feel the throat constrict if the Chakra closes up under the assault of a negative environment.

★ Headaches.

Often caused by excessive activity at the level of the ego, for example too much thinking, planning or worrying. To help soothe away the pain we can look at a candle flame during our meditation, or hold our right palm over the forehead and say to ourselves 'I forgive' several times. By saying 'I forgive', we are trying to drop the mental baggage which may be fuelling the thoughts.

We can also gently massage Sandalwood Oil into the front Agnya with the fingers. If the pain is at the back of the head, we can stroke from the left temple back and downwards across the back of the head with the right hand to bring down the inflated super ego and so help soothe the pain.

★ Sore Eyes
To help our eyes, we should take time out to look at the sky or parts of nature such as trees or green grass. This is also a very effective counterbalance for too much reading, computing or other close quarter work.

We can also try to help our eyes stay fresh by not allowing our attention to flit from place to place too much in general. A stable and steady attention is a happy attention.

★ Throat.
Try to protect the throat against extreme cold, dust or even excessive talking. Where possible use a scarf. Chewing raw liquorice or eating honey can also help with problems here. Again this area is governed by the Vishuddhi Chakra, so we can follow those guidelines too.

★ Insomnia.
This is a problem of an over active right side channel. For this we need to balance ourselves in the meditation so as to cool down the right side. A cool water and salt footsoak is also recommended during the evening meditation.

★ Hot Liver.
This is also caused by an over exerted right side. One of the symptoms is a fragmented attention, so that we find it hard to meditate and become irritable, restless or ill at ease. We can use the ice pack to cool down the liver area directly, and try and avoid eating heating things like fried foods, alcohol or caffeine for a few days until the heat subsides.

Sahaja Yoga and the treatment of more serious ailments

There are a number of medical studies underway which are researching the potential for combating more serious ailments using Sahaja Yoga meditation techniques.

So far the research is in its early stages, although Dr Ramesh Ramocha of the Natural Therapies Unit at the Royal Hospital for Women in Sydney, Australia, has recently reported on a pilot study[viii] which suggest that this form of meditation may have a beneficial role to play in the treatment of menopausal hot flushes, severe migraine and psychological stress. According to Dr Manocha, the meditation may reduce the release of catecholamines and other stress hormones and increase beneficial parasympathetic activity.

In another study, Dr Guy B Marks and colleagues at the Institute of Respiratory Medicine in Australia randomly assigned some 50 people with asthma to undertake Sahaja Yoga meditation in comparison with a group that practiced other relaxation methods, mental exercises and engaged in group discussions. The results showed that the people in the meditation group had a greater reduction in airway sensitiveness – which is the tendency to close up – than those in the comparison group. The yoga group also reported a larger decrease in tension and tiredness.[ix]

Other studies conducted in India also suggest that Sahaja Yoga can be beneficial in treating epilepsy and hypertension, whilst work recently completed in the UK by clinical psychologist Dr Adam Morgan, has demonstrated that significant benefits can arise from the use of Sahaja Yoga meditation to treat patients suffering from anxiety and depression.

These international studies are just a small part of a worldwide initiative to identify and demonstrate the powerful physical benefits of practicing this ancient form of meditation. Whilst it is still too early to talk confidently in terms of 'breakthrough' treatment, these results are beginning to draw the attention of the international medical community to the very real benefits of this form of meditation.

As further proof of this growing interest, several influential bodies such as the National Institutes of Health in the US have started to conduct official Sahaja Yoga programmes as part of their evaluation of holistic healthcare and meditation[x]. In addition several doctors who themselves practice Sahaja Yoga are continuing to research the subject, and a number of them have already gained their degree qualifications by submitting theses on the topic of Sahaja Yoga meditation and medicinal treatment.

SELF KNOWLEDGE

Self knowledge is not merely a mental concept of who we are, it is a deep rooted understanding. Most of us have an idea of the type of people we are, or think we are, but these ideas are usually based around a set of conditionings and mental concepts which we have accumulated over time. We may think of ourselves as goal oriented, efficient, lazy, happy go lucky or any number of alternatives. However, these words only touch on the outermost levels of our personality. In order to understand ourselves fully we need to go much deeper into our spiritual being and gain a true spiritual insight which goes way beyond the mental stage. These insights are the key feature of our self knowledge, and it is these fundamental aspects that we need to grasp in order to succeed in our spiritual quest.

Self knowledge is the ultimate truth, and while to some it may seem an unattainable goal in these modern times, there are definite milestones which prove that we can achieve more than we ever thought possible. There are a million books written about the subject, and we are constantly bombarded by magazine and television reports showing us how to 'find the inner you'. In truth however, almost all of them are simply pandering to our ego, to make us feel better about ourselves.

These upbeat items usually tell us how much better we are than we believe, and offer a selection of trendy sound-bites which, like

156

fad diets, are supposed to help us attain that all important self improvement. We're told that if we follow the handy tips we will get a better job, a happier relationship, and our lives will improve beyond all belief.

Just like the diet of the month, however, these are all artificial solutions, generated to sell more product rather than to genuinely help us evolve. The fact is that real self improvement can only come from hard work, generally over many years. There are no quick fixes, and we should realise that the process will highlight some pretty uncomfortable things about ourselves that we would probably prefer not to face. But there is no shortcut; if you want to lose weight, then you have to eat properly and eat less. End of story. In the same way, if we genuinely – there's that word again – want to evolve spiritually and attain real self knowledge, then we have to work for it.

So what is self knowledge exactly, and how do we know when we've got it? Well, the ancients knew it as complete awareness of who and what we are, and how we fit into the universe we inhabit. At a minimum it proves without a doubt that we are more than just a body and mind, muscle and bone. It delves into the deepest corners of our psyche and reveals all the innermost secrets of our desires, conditionings, emotions, characteristics, tendencies and ego. You can see why it can be painful for some people to go there unprepared.

The process of meditation opens up the door to these insights as a natural part of our spiritual growth. This is because we can only hope to evolve if we have a firm foundation from which to launch our journey, and that means knowing who we really are and what we are really capable of achieving. It's no good thinking that we can easily meditate our way to being a more loving person if we are unaware that we still have a closed and fearful heart. We need to flush the problem out, face it, deal with it and wash it away before moving on.

157

This is why the meditation is so vital. The problem with simply reading a book on self-improvement is that reading is the easy part. We can all nod sagely and agree with an author who tells us that we need to stop feeling guilty for the past. This is clearly a sensible thing and easy to accept. However what is not so easy is actually translating those words into a reality. Some books suggest that we can achieve a result through the power of positive thinking – the 'every day I am becoming a more dynamic and forgiving person' school of learning.

Again, like fad diets, these mind games may work for a short while, but then their power starts to fade away and we once more find ourselves battling our demons and fears. Back to square one. Self help groups are also another popular way of tackling the task, as there's no doubt that sharing problems definitely makes it easier to deal with them. It's the same with psychotherapy, counselling and a dozen other modern solutions to an age old problem.

But they all fail in one crucial way - they cannot deal with the source of our problems. Only genuine yoga meditation – and it's hard not to sound like an advert here – can cleanse the crucial subtle Chakra system, energise our spiritual energies and help us really change in every way, physically, mentally, emotionally. Without addressing the source of the problem, our spiritual makeup, all other treatments are bound to fail eventually.

Whatever we do on a physical and mental level is doomed to anchor us to that state. It is only when we do as the truly ancient wise men did and transcend the material plane, that we can let the eternal spirit in us take us on a higher journey. How can this be proved? Well take a look at the movement for peace across the world. Since civilisation began, man has been fighting without cease. There have been religions formed, treaties signed, peace organisations founded and all we have succeeded in doing is moving wars from the battlefield to impotent international forums and then back to the battle field again.

158

Man has become adept with tools and technology to an extent that is absolutely astounding, but in real terms – especially relating to our attitude to others who share this small planet with us – we are still in the dark ages. Here we are in the 21st century and children are still dying because they can't get a drink of proper pure water? It's simply disgusting! Meanwhile the aid agencies fight egotistical and political wars to score points, and battle for funding and recognition in a world where the power of oil speaks louder than the cry of a dying child.

So self knowledge is critically needed today more than ever, so that we can move our 'civilisation' onto a new level and let it fulfil its potential. This begins with each and every one of us. If we can each start to sincerely and diligently turn our face away from mere material gain and look towards self improvement, then we can and will change society beyond all recognition. It sounds like a worn out new age lament, but that doesn't make it any the less real.

Once we start to meditate and fearlessly face ourselves with a view to improving, we begin a process which can literally take us anywhere we want to go. Self mastery through meditation gives us the power to make the kind of tough decisions that are good for our own evolution, as well as our society's well-being. We learn to be less afraid, more willing to challenge the 'herd mentality' and better able to distinguish right from wrong, truth from lies, reality from illusion.

We are able to contribute wisdom to our environment without ego getting in the way. As we begin to learn who we are, so too do we recognise the reality of others around us, which gives us the chance to help them in the most effective way possible. Most importantly, we find the courage to stand up and be counted as a spiritual person in a world which has cynically dismissed spirituality as a minority new age trend which is not to be taken too seriously.

Above all, self-knowledge is about realising the truth. Whether it be about the nature of God and the universe, or about our distaste

159

for fried food. And the critical thing to remember about truth is that it is a power that cannot be defeated. It can be concealed for a while, but eventually it always, always emerges triumphant.

VIBRATIONS

A powerful and unmistakeable sign that we are beginning to reap the benefit of our meditation is our growing sensitivity to the vibrational universe around us. When we first start out this ability is somewhat fragile. We are not sure whether we are truly feeling a real 'sixth sense' or whether we are deluding ourselves or being misled by our environment. It's a common confusion.

But after a while we begin to recognise the different aspects of the vibrations and how they fit in with all the teachings of Sahaja Yoga in every way. This new sensitivity then gradually becomes an indispensable part of everyday life. We use it to examine the state of our subtle system and work on ourselves to clear obstructions on the Chakras. We use it to evaluate situations, environments, our relationships and encounters, and we learn to use it naturally, in the same way that you would check a barometer to watch for rain.

Where at first we may be faltering and doubtful of our vibrational abilities, after a time we gain confidence and start to trust the results more and more. This is because the vibrations we feel are really nothing more than an extension of our subtle system, and as our subtle system gets stronger so too does our vibrational awareness. The coolness we feel on our fingers, hands and body is an indication of well-being and comfort passed to us from the spiritual realm. Vibrations are involuntary, we do not and cannot control their appearance or disappearance. One minute we may be sitting on a bus as normal, the next we can feel the most incredible rush of coolness as we pass a spiritually significant location or encounter an ancient soul.

It is the involuntary nature of this vibratory awareness that makes it such a useful friend. Because it happens spontaneously without our conscious effort, we learn to trust it for what it is, a genuinely benevolent and powerful guide.

LOVE AND COMPASSION

What do we know about being open hearted? We may certainly understand what the media portrays as love; it is two people finding each other attractive, falling in love and marrying in one episode (after a small yet entertaining bust up, of course). For many people, this simplistic chain of events is their ultimate dream, and of course they are often disappointed when things don't turn out exactly as they had hoped, and the dream fades away under an onslaught of bickering or misunderstanding.

The heart is the seat of our love and home to our compassion. However all too often we are afraid to open up and allow these wonderful qualities to flow as they should. We hide behind our fears, doubts and ambitions, displaying a false mask to the world to avoid being hurt. The result is a society based on illusion, hidden behind ego and posturing, never truly communicating as human being to human being. Small wonder then that the divorce rate is so high in the modern world, and that relationships come and go as the wind blows.

Meditation opens up the blocked channels of the heart and helps us lose the fear of judgment and rejection. We become givers, not takers. We look for excuses to exercise our compassion, instead of avoiding commitment. We stop worrying about being taken advantage of, or looking naïve and other imaginary scenarios which we may have used in the past to avoid opening our private shell. Instead we begin to live as the person we really are, with our faults, loves, enthusiasms and strengths on full show to the world.

Love and compassion don't just point to a nice personality. In their most potent form they provide a power that is strong enough to defeat legions of negativity and personal decay. The truly compassionate heart forgives instantly, and so moves beyond the cage of the past into the glory of the moment. The loving heart

161

cannot judge, for love is truly blind. Our yoga lets us see people for how they can be, with their full potential glowing like a beacon.

After we have been meditating for some time, we notice that our hard edged shell starts to flake away, melted by the force of the loving spirit.. Sometimes this can be just a little disconcerting, as we venture out into the world of trust and hope, leaving behind suspicion and doubt. But after a while we start to realise that we no longer flinch and suffer, even when we are cruelly rebuffed by insensitive souls. Instead we brush off setbacks instantly through the balance of our yoga; we forgive and move on, anxious to engineer the next encounter in our voyage of discovery.

As our heart grows stronger, so too does our faith. We really begin to understand the power of true self-knowledge and to trust our instincts to lead us where we should be heading. The harsh uncertainties of life start fading away into the background, as we step forward with a spring and a smile. Of course it's not all plain sailing, and there are times when even the hardiest practitioner can experiences a severe jolt; a family blow, unexpected illness, even death. But these events increasingly lose their ability to seriously knock us off balance for any length of time, and in most cases actually make us stronger spiritually and emotionally.

We begin to learn what true love is. Not the stuff of the cheap novel, but the combination of friendship, trust, respect and support which are at its core. Love doesn't just flare up in an instant, like infatuation or lust. Love grows slowly and tenderly over time, deepening as we start to learn more about the object of our affection. Love does not demand anything, it is marvellously unselfish. In the same way that a mother only wants to give love to her newborn child, those who are experiencing true love think only of serving their relationship.

If we are always looking for a reciprocal reaction, or constantly demand attention, then we are not experiencing real love at all. If we allow suspicion, jealousy and negligence to enter into our relationships, then we poison the well of love and destroy the portal to our compassion. It is a cliché, but it still holds true - love is pure.

The rewards from the opening of our heart through true yoga meditation are many, but the biggest is the contentment that comes from realising that we can love and fully be loved in the midst of what seems to be a cynical world. Our heart adores peace and our whole spiritual being responds to the power of love when it is flowing properly. There is nothing that can stand in the way of a loving heart; no suspicion, anger or fear. At last we discover what it is like to be truly free.

SELF ESTEEM AND SELF RESPECT

There are over 60,000 books dealing with the subject of self esteem on the global Amazon.com bookstore, and another 105,000 covering self improvement. So it's probably fair to say that we in the modern world have a bit of a problem with self confidence. At best the problem makes us hesitant, shy and secretive, at worst it drives those at the fringe to become reclusive sociopaths or worse. And the greatest irony is that it is the industrial powerhouses of the modern age, the Western countries, which have the biggest share of the problem. Despite economically and culturally ruling over most of the civilised globe, we still have a hard time believing in ourselves. Or maybe that's the reason in itself.

We are brought up in a world which teaches us that we have to win at all costs. We are constantly appraised for performance almost before we can walk and talk, and every step of our childhood is dogged by tests, examinations and a constant flow of expectations. No wonder that by the time we reach our teenage years we can start to feel alienated and a little overwhelmed. Many of us, of course, adjust to the reality of a competitive world. We make do the best way we can. We struggle, jostle and finally find a level that we can feel comfortable with - in relationships, career and life in general.

But somehow deep down perhaps we are not as comfortable or secure as we appear on the surface. It's hard to be comfortable with who you are in a society that worships unrealistic standards – fame, beauty, celebrity, power. Surgically enhanced superstars from stage, screen, sports field and catwalk define the role models for our age. Never mind that they live on a diet of total self absorption or battle obsessively to prop up their fragile egos, we still feel inadequate unless we can match their physical attributes and media celebrated personality. Children are brought up to venerate sports stars and television personalities rather than wise members of our society. We are cajoled into trying to emulate the shallow and empty lives of people who are lauded for simply being famous. Indeed a strange situation.

Nevertheless, one fact remains fundamentally true. Not a single one of the 165,000 self improvement books, nor any of the thousands of lecturers, counsellors, psychiatrists or media experts can make us become better people, not even if we attend every help group, read every book and practice every fashionable technique. They may be able to help us adjust mentally to our condition, to accept who we are. They may also be able to help us become more positive in outlook and more determined to overcome our feelings of inadequacy, but in the end we will still be who we are until the day we die. Unless….

Unless we realise that the only way for us to really improve ourselves as human beings, in every single way possible, is to transform through our spiritual dimension. We must become yogis; we must transform ourselves from Homo Sapien to Homo Spiritus. This may come across as a hugely grandiose and pretentious statement, but it is the truth. Any other form of improvement is inevitably destined to fail, simply because it is a product of our mental processes and not of our spirit and soul. Unless and until we experience a fundamental change in our spiritual being, we can never really cut ourselves free from the cage of our emotions, desires and conditionings. Never.

Even the so called spiritual approaches to self improvement, involving traditional or modern religions and practices are doomed to failure unless they activate the most fundamental catalyst of human change, the Kundalini; and do so in an auspicious and proper manner. This is not mysterious, it is simply because every true yoga requires that this process occurs, and real yoga is the evolution of humankind in action. For the individual this means that at last there is a real and proven method of self improvement which works, and does not involve drugs, trauma or debilitating treatments.

Of course yoga is not an instant 'quick-fix' solution and no-one is claiming that the results can be guaranteed for every individual. As with everything, we get out of it what we put in. But for those who persevere, the results can be truly astonishing. For example, any problems we may have with low self esteem and guilt begin to disappear immediately we understand the reality of the spiritual cosmos. It's hard to keep punishing ourselves when we realise that we are such a small part of this huge eternal universe. We also start to realise that we don't have to try and be anyone else, that self knowledge is a far more important goal.

There's also a group of people who through a sort of twisted logic believe that they are not worthy or 'ready' to undertake a journey of self discovery. Despite the fact that they recognise the power of yoga to help their lives, they cannot overcome the lack of self esteem which makes them feel that they cannot achieve anything from the practice of meditation. This is of course a complete myth, an illusion which plays through their left Vishuddhi and Agnya Chakras, and which can easily be overcome through simply ignoring the negative thoughts and continuing with the practice. Once we start meditating, these thoughts will start to disappear as our system clears.

The cleansing action of our Kundalini on our Heart Chakra gives us the strength to face ourselves and realise just how powerful we can become if we allow our yoga to grow stronger, and this too

165

helps us walk away from the illusion of personal inadequacy. If we are succeeding in growing through Sahaja Yoga, then we must have some integral value which makes us a worthwhile member of the world. Of course even after we have been meditating for some time, we may have doubts and fears, but we learn to witness them and by so doing detach ourselves from the worst of their effects. It is the start of our liberation.

Instead of focussing on our imagined faults, we focus instead on how to improve ourselves through meditation and introspection. We all have faults, but that doesn't automatically mean we're bad people. We have to overcome the negativity that tells us we cannot improve, that we are stuck with our problems for ever. Sahaja Yoga gives us a way out of that cage and lets us soar free on the back of our winged spiritual carriage. In particular we stop feeling guilty for things that we may have done in the past or even imaginary things that we have been carrying around with us.

We learn that making mistakes is human, we all do it. And we learn that we either let them dog our footsteps for the rest of our lives, or we move on and make sure we avoid those same mistakes in the future. With our newly enlightened attention we also begin to see things clearer, and find it easier to differentiate between right and wrong actions.

One of the key benefits of the introspection that comes from meditation, is that we come to terms with our relationships in all forms. We forgive ourselves for our childhood, and we forgive our parents for anything they may have done – knowingly or unknowingly – to us when we were growing up.

Self respect is about believing in ourselves, but not merely on a mental level. It has to be a rock solid core of our being, which says 'hey I'm not perfect, but I'm getting somewhere, and through the power of my spiritual adventure I can see the fruits of my yoga growing all the time.'

REMOVING FEAR

The dictionary defines fear thus: *A painful emotion, apprehension, anxiety, dread.*

Whatever the cause, however much the degree, we all feel fear. In many ways we are brought up to live in uneasy familiarity with our fears. When we're youngsters, barely able to walk we are taught to fear strangers, to be careful of what we do, eat or say. The pressures continue in this way while we grow to adulthood. We learn to fear examinations, to fear failing in our career, and as we age we begin to dread our inevitable fate – illness and death.

It is little wonder then that already by the time we are young adults we can feel burdened by the weight of what seems to be a thousand years. But the fact is that fear is not an inevitable part of life, it is something that we acquire through environment and conditionings.

It is also something that is reinforced for commercial gain by everyone from insurance services to politicians anxious to gain our support. It is a tool to keep us in line and make us malleable consumers, employees and citizens. But we can live without it.

The root of fear

On the physical side fear is the outcome of a fervent imagination, yet another mental process. We rarely have time to indulge in anxious thoughts when we are actually faced with a crisis, it is only when we have the time to think that we become apprehensive. However, if we can take a detached view of our fearful thoughts, then we can often overcome them in a real and effective way.

Unfortunately we spend much of our time thinking about the past and the future, and we spend very little time just living in the present moment, enjoying the now. It is this constant oscillation between a past we cannot control and a future which has not happened yet which fuels most of our fears.

To combat these illusory states, we have to learn through our introspection how to remain in the present, with our focus on the now. If we can do that, then a huge and anxious weight can be lifted from our shoulders permanently.

Our fear inducing environment.

a) We may be constantly worried about our job, the relationship with our boss or the security of our position. This anxiety increases with age, as we become more concerned about maintaining the comfort of our adult family lifestyle. Fear of our job security is used as a means of keeping us productive and acquiescent, even in the face of factors we may be uncomfortable with.

b) We are constantly told that we need to secure our future, to plan for our old age and even ensure that our children and loved ones are cared for. Of course there is nothing inherently wrong about this viewpoint, but when it is constantly brought to our attention by dramatic insurance and medical advertising and sensational media material, then it can start to wear us down. Subconsciously we begin to worry about everything that **might** happen to us, no matter how outlandish or remote a possibility. Small wonder that we become so easily stressed.

c) The health business is booming, fed in large part by our media fuelled unease with the perils of our modern world. Every day we are told that one product or another causes heart disease or cancer, or that some activity is good or bad for us, or that we need to be on this type of diet or another. These emotional attacks help to sell drugs and cures and also help to drive home the message that we are all reliant on the status quo to keep us from falling ill and being a burden on society and family.

d) We live in fear of ruining our relationships. Divorce threatens one in two families, children and parents undergo classic symptoms of the generation gap, and we read of the dysfunction that is an everyday part of many high pressure, stress oriented lifestyles. And so we grow more anxious, seek counselling, consume drugs to calm

168

us down and generally succumb to a life where anxiety, and its attendant symptoms, are an everyday reality.

What can meditation do?

There are many aspects of meditation which help us to fight and overcome our fears and anxieties, on every level of our being. On the physical side our meditation gives us a space where we can take time to introspect and reflect on our lives, where we can seek solace in a peaceful moment amongst the hubbub. On an emotional level, by meditating we start to become more balanced in everything we do, as our Chakras become clear and the energies start to flow properly around our subtle system.

Our spiritual being is also enhanced as we grow deeper in our meditation. The flow of energy and the work of the Kundalini encourages a greater understanding of our place in the universe, gives us a sense of perspective with regard to the world we inhabit and helps us to distance ourselves from the day to day trivia which can often bring us down and increase our anxiety.

Every time we meditate, and more of the Kundalini energy flows through our subtle system, nourishing and cleansing, we become more 'enlightened'. On a practical level our Heart Chakra, the seat of our sense of courage and fearlessness, opens and these 'lion hearted' qualities start to manifest in our everyday experiences. As this Chakra opens, we begin to take charge of our lives and make difficult decisions which we would perhaps otherwise avoid through fear of making a mistake. We begin to have faith in ourselves and in our ability to tread the right path.

Practical Steps

i) Once we start to meditate, we should examine our actions and reactions and note how we change over time. Keep a diary and jot down unusual events and personal behaviour which show a change in our approach to life.

ii) Take note of reactions to events. Do we still, after a while, become anxious when faced with a potential problem way ahead in the future, or have we started to take things as they come?

iii) Are we becoming more decisive in our actions and decisions? After we have been meditating for a while we should be able to make more focussed decisions whilst worrying less about any imaginary potential failure in the future.

iv) Are we sleeping better, do we awake more refreshed and without that familiar stab of anxiety we may have felt in the past? Eventually we should be able to sleep soundly in the midst of the most strenuous circumstances.

v) Watch yourself in the midst of a threatening situation. Do we take a step back from the confrontation and examine the situation dispassionately? If so, this is a sign that the meditation is beginning to develop that all important sense of detachment, which is crucial to maintaining a balanced lifestyle.

Conclusion

Fear is not an inevitable part of our lifestyle. It was Franklin D Roosevelt, on the occasion of his US Presidential inauguration in 1933, who said '*the only thing we have to fear is fear itself*' and nowhere is this more clearly exemplified than in our pre and post meditation lives.

Once we can feel comfortable with ourselves for who we are, and once we have settled into the state of balance that comes from being a calmer and more focussed individual, we will be able to take advantage of all that life has to offer without irrational fear of consequences. Anxieties over the future will be gone and in its place will be the enthusiasm and joy that comes from living every day to its fullest, no matter what the circumstances.

REMOVING ANGER

Anger destroys. It ruins lives, relationships, careers, personalities. It scars children and friendships, and eats away at the soul. No-one would deny that it is a thing to be avoided, but unfortunately everywhere we turn we see evidence of the anger which lurks inside the human psyche. Newspaper and television reports are constantly filled with talk of angry groups and individuals; all of them infuriated by some real or perceived injustice or insult.

People are routinely described as 'outraged' or 'furious', whilst little attention is paid to voices of conciliation or modesty. Critics vent their wrath on features to which they take exception; bad meals, bad art, rotten holidays. We seem to be fascinated by anger and rage and at the same time intimidated by it. It is the modern bogeyman. Terrorists use anger and rage as their weapon of fear, and it works insofar as it creates a climate of suspicion and mistrust in their target societies.

Yogis understand the reasons for the anger in modern times, and battle constantly to overcome this destructive emotion. In its mildest form, of course, anger is called irritation, and we know it to be a symptom of an over heated right side. Maybe even a hot liver, which is having difficulty accomplishing all its purifying tasks. For the yoga practitioner, the focus is on cooling down the right side and looking after the liver by eating well, avoiding exposure to stressful situations and focussing on nature as often as possible.

Over time, the yogi becomes more immune to the triggers that would normally set off an anger attack, although even the most balanced being can find it hard not to react to injustice, bullying or ignorant aggression. Under normal circumstances severe exposure to triggers like this can cause the Agnya Chakra to constrict, and from there we can find ourselves arguing, thinking angry thoughts or losing the power to forgive. We may even get a headache too.

When this happens we know that strong measures have to be taken to fight off this over-heating of our right side. The more balanced we are, the easier it is for us to stay calm, even when facing the worst of circumstances. One of the hardest situations to deal with is where the yoga practitioner is caught up in a hostile environment not of their making, for instance chatting with an angry boss or friend over the telephone, or dealing with an irate customer at work.

In these circumstances it is important to realise that the problem is not ours, but one that we are helping to work out with our subtle attention. It will probably feel very unpleasant, exactly the same as being angry yourself, but the difference is that we can look at the feelings dispassionately with our enlightened attention, and by so doing we can take remedial action to cool down as soon as possible. When faced with cases of this type we should always try to withdraw from the conversation or scene as soon as we can, in order to avoid even more exposure to the negative vibrations that we are sucking in.

We can then take a few moments to sit quietly and with our attention bring ourselves back to the centre by focussing on the Sahasrara Chakra at the top of the head. In severe cases we should try and have a relaxing, cool footsoak, where we place our feet in a bowl of lightly salted water while meditating. This effectively sucks the negativity out of our lower Chakras and makes it easier for us to cool down our whole subtle system properly.

In extreme cases, where for instance we have been exposed to a long bout of anger, hostility or aggression, we can try and use the power of nature to help us clear out, perhaps by visiting a nearby park to sit on the grass whilst contemplating the simplicity of nature around us. It sounds terribly 'new age', but this kind of treatment is incredibly powerful and one which most people instinctively recognise in times of stress in their lives. In olden times, people often travelled to the seaside to recover after a period of trauma in their lives. Salt, water and an ocean view are a powerfully healing combination.

The key thing to remember is that as yoga practitioners we no longer have to be slaves to anger and its cousins. We now have the power to corral these negative emotions and dissolve them through meditation and gentle attention. Just as importantly, we learn to

172

recognise the onset of these potentially destructive feelings as soon as they start to manifest, when they're easiest to combat. Such is the power of our attention, that even the slightest sign of irritability or agitation is enough to flag a warning to us that we need to take early corrective action.

There are those, of course, for whom a hot liver is a fact of life. These people may have been damaged through excesses in their youth, or may just carry a faulty gene which has caused the problem. The main symptom is a constant barrage of thinking, thoughts cascading through the mind in an unceasing stream. In extreme cases they may also be very judgemental about people and things around them. They are picky people, nothing satisfies them and they are always getting into confrontational scenes with people around them.

For these people, meditation often opens up a whole new world and introduces a novel concept – peace. Once they manage to soothe their liver and right side down, they can begin to enjoy a life of satisfaction, without rancour, snappiness or that permanent cantankerous attitude that has probably marked their life out before. It's certainly not an instant cure, nothing genuine ever is, but if they are patient and continue to meditate with full focus, they will notice a significant improvement in the overall quality of their lives and relationships.

Anger destroys, yoga rebuilds!

- CHAPTER SIX -

The life which is unexamined is not worth living. Socrates.

GOING DEEPER IN OUR YOGA

We have seen earlier that we meditate to attain self knowledge and go deeper in our spiritual awareness. But what exactly does that mean? Well, as with everything to do with our yoga, the answer comes in a number of layers. On the first level, going deeper indicates that we are becoming more aware of our spiritual nature and are more in tune with the universe in which we live. This new awareness gives us that wonderful feeling of peace when we are totally in balance. This awareness also helps us to recognise when we need to learn from an event, and drives us on to search for the truth in every corner of our life.

Going deeper also means that on a more basic level we are able to experience more intense meditations, with prolonged bouts of thoughtless awareness. And on yet another level we know that we are going deeper when we start to impress others with our gravitas, balanced approach to life and generally untroubled demeanour. However, in the end, going deeper really only means one thing, that we are evolving. Changing and improving ourselves to become a better, more spiritual person.

Evolution

What does evolution mean? Is it something that we should really concern ourselves with, or is it just for those poor unhappy souls who are looking for answers to impossible questions? In fact evolution is an absolutely vital and natural part of life. Every living creature has to undergo a continual process of evolution or their

174

species will eventually stagnate and become extinct. Man is no exception.

The difference with man is that we have a sense of self awareness which is a unique and vital part of the human process. Because of this conscious mind, we have the option to walk along a completely new evolutionary path, one which can lead us away from our traditional 'tool-using' materialism and leads towards our spiritual liberation.

We have arrived at a clear fork in the path to our future. One direction leads to an increasingly constricted material existence and the other points towards the final liberation of humanity through the ultimate spiritual communion. Those who stay on the material road will inevitably continue to suffer from the problems which come from individualism and social isolation. Unless we can rediscover the power of universal brotherhood, we are doomed to perpetuate the cycle of war and violence that has plagued civilisation since the first hominids walked the earth.

The spiritual route – towards Homo Spiritus if you will – offers the only real light of hope for humanity, to lead human society to its full potential. Unless we can find a way to change our innate personality and character, and become more peaceful, responsible and mature we will never stand a chance of changing the world for the better. The only way to transform society as a whole is to transform the individual first.

So in these terms, we can see that this important journey of spiritual evolution really does represent a crucial opportunity for us to radically reform our universe. This reformation will allow us to enter into an age where brotherhood, love and understanding will become a part of our everyday experience. It may sound somewhat melodramatic, but this is probably the last chance for mankind to rediscover its purpose and return once more to the pure enjoyment of the glory of life.

Will everyone 'get it'? Clearly not. In the same way that large numbers of a species die out during periods of evolutionary turmoil, so too, many people will not be able to overcome their natural antipathy, laziness or ignorance and grasp the opportunity that is on offer. This is the nature of things.

It helps to remember also that the opposite of evolution in this instance is decay. We cannot remain in a fixed state in life, any more than we can expect to live forever and not grow old. If we cannot progress, then we will degenerate. It is interesting to note that almost all of the great civilisations of the past, Roman, Greek, British, Ottoman, Austro-Hungarian, and so on, have flared into being, peaked fairly rapidly and then degenerated back into a general state of disrepair. Decadence, corruption and complacency always seem to quickly follow on from any peak of civilised society.

The choice is clear. Either we recognise the signs of a civilisation at the cusp of a momentous shift in existence, or we ignore the signals and spiral headlong into chaos and uncertainty. Once the process has started it cannot be turned back until it is over. Once the fish started to emerge from the oceans onto land, there was no going back to the sea.

Trial

To round itself out, life calls not for perfection but for completeness; and for this the 'thorn in the flesh' is needed, the suffering of defects without which there is no progress and no ascent. Carl Jung.

We evolve through tests. The ancients knew them as tapasya, and we perhaps may know of them as penance or ordeal. Whichever term we use, the end result is the same, we grow in spirituality. It may seem strange to suggest that we mainly progress through pain, but there is a logic to it which makes much more sense once we understand exactly what these tests are.

Although we may not realise it, every single day we perform an act of penance or trial. When we rise from our bed in the morning,

176

we are leaving a place of comfort and warmth and venturing out, probably to work. This simple act of leaving a comfortable position to perform our daily duties is a form of trial. We need to have the motivation and the will to get up. We have to be resolute about leaving the home no matter what the weather, and of course we often find ourselves heading towards a job that may not provide everything that we would wish for in a career.

These factors all combine to create a series of tests that we need to pass if we are to survive the day and our lives on this earth. Many people, however, equate the concept of trial with something either physically, psychologically or emotionally painful. They think that trial is nothing more than suffering and the negation of pleasure.

Thankfully it's not as black and white as that, so perhaps we should examine this point in more detail. Of course going to work definitely can involve some suffering, but on the other hand for many of us our daily task also provides some real comfort and enjoyment. We meet colleagues, enjoy challenges, and are mentally stimulated for at least a part of our working day. So in reality most of the suffering is at a very low level, and in many cases we may not even notice it. In the same way that we may not notice that we lightly grazed our arm on the bathroom wall in the morning. These ordeals then are clearly not significant in terms of our personal evolution. Or are they?

If these minor forms of trial don't count, what exactly does? What is true tapasya and how is it quantified? Aggressive behaviour from others, a death in the family, career crises, money problems – these are all events which could be classed as unpleasant, problems which make life harder. But few people again would see them as spiritually significant. In fact many people would say that the objective of spiritual practice is to banish these types of events from our lives. However in reality all tests are important, and even the most mundane example has a rightful place in our journey of self discovery.

The fact is that we cannot grow spiritually unless we are willing to face ourselves, our ego and conditionings and our baggage in general. We must also be prepared to undergo change and enjoy the process as it happens. All of these factors require some pretty tough decisions and actions. Few have trouble dealing with the smaller problems, they just seem to take care of themselves, but it's the larger issues that we fear, anything that can cause us pain.

It is for this reason that we face difficult events in our lives even after we start meditating seriously, events which can seem quite hard to deal with. Each of us has a different concept of difficult, though, don't we. For one person, an untrustworthy boss may be almost unbearable, whilst another will just grin and bear it and get on with life. This is why each of the tests we face after our self-realisation and during our spiritual ascent is tailor made – divinely customised, you might say – to our personal needs.

Remember that every one of us undergoes continual tests of character every day, so those events which are designed to move us higher have to be of sufficient weight to rise above the norm. It sounds like a divinely inspired torture program, but in reality it turns out to be something sublime rather than horrid. Because after a while we begin to recognise the nature of the tests when they arise. Our enlightened attention – remember that little feature? – helps us spot the clues very quickly.

We immediately recognise the reason why we need to be tested financially if we have always had a problem looking after money in our life. We recognise the nature of a test in a relationship if we know that we need to become more detached as a person. The tests may come continually, but after a while they start to resemble a game of chess, with the divine process posing tricky questions for us to unravel and solve before we move on to the next level of play.

It is a common fallacy that the life of a yogi is one of simple retreat, contemplation and peace. These are certainly part of the overall goal, but the ultimate aim is not just to practice our yoga, but to become our yoga. And in order to achieve that state we need to become so detached about regular day to day events and trials, that our balance stays rock steady no matter what situation we face.

This is probably one of the hardest things to explain to someone who has just started practicing Sahaja Yoga, since they will probably have begun doing the meditation primarily to get away from a stressful lifestyle. And then they are told that they should expect to regularly face difficulties as part of the process of becoming more peaceful? It doesn't make sense.

But in fact it does make sense. In the same way that animals need to evolve through trial, we also cannot ascend spiritually unless we are challenged and overcome that challenge. The worse thing that can happen to a yogi is to become too comfortable in their life. Comfort eventually leads to complacency, and that in turn leads to the ruination of everything spiritual. Our ego starts to fool us, we lose the ability to discriminate between right and wrong, and pretty soon we find ourselves making excuses as to why we don't have to bother too much about self improvement anyway.

On the other hand, when we face a stiff test, we have to rise above it in order to triumph. That's the only way we can drop the baggage holding us down and move on up. For many of us this process can take a long while, and we may face and fail the same test time and again in different forms. But at the heart of the ordeal will be the same benevolent objective – to help us overcome some buried negative issue that is impeding our spiritual progress. Money, relationships, guilt, self respect, domination of others. The list is endless and each of us has our own recipe for success that we must cook up in order to triumph over the process.

People sometimes have a problem reconciling this apparently turbulent process with the idea that the spiritual path is one of peace, tranquillity and harmony. How can the two exist together? The answer is a little complex. The fact is that we can never experience true peace of the spirit unless we learn to be detached about worldly affairs. The Buddha said categorically that desires are the real cause of unhappiness, and that we can only overcome our unhappiness once we lose our earthly desires.

Desires of course do not just mean that we want a new car or coat. They also take the form of a desire for a particular outcome to a situation or event. Say we decide to go to the movies. We may hope that the movie is good, and that we will not have to queue too long in order to get in. By having these desires we start a chain of events that can only end in one of two ways – either we will be disappointed in the events that occur, or we will be happy for a while until the next situation takes our attention.

This constant and debilitating process of need, desire, gratification or disappointment lies at the heart of all that is wrong with the material and worldly lifestyle. We cannot help but experience anger, sorrow, disappointment, anguish and pain if our desires are not met. But these emotions are direct competitors to the contentment, peace and fulfilment that we seek in our spiritual journey. And so we have to learn to move beyond the constant flow of desires into a space where we are indifferent to the outcome of situations or events.

This sounds like a recipe for disaster, a passionless place where we experience no real joy, but in fact it is the reverse. This kind of detached contentment liberates us from so much of the pain of the world, that we can do nothing else but enjoy. And in fact we do practice this kind of detachment every day. When we open the fridge door in the morning we will see a variety of situations. Some days there might be more milk in the bottle, and on others less. We don't become annoyed if the bottle is only half instead of three quarters full. Because it doesn't really matter, does it?

So let's move the stakes up a little. Many of us will be quite happy if our commuter train runs a little slowly one morning on our way to work. Others will be totally stressed out and become agitated. Here we see the same situation causing different responses,

180

which shows that we can choose how to respond if we want to. A test is only a test if we are affected by it. Once we pass a test and no longer worry about that particular thing, it can no longer cause us anguish any more than a half full bottle of milk can. We become detached from the outcome.

For example, truly detached yogis do not care if they have to wait somewhere for one, two or ten hours at a time. They have no place else they would rather be. For them time is not a test. For most of us in this modern hectic world, waiting an hour is an almost unbearable chore, after which we start taking steps to shorten or circumvent the wait. If, however, through our meditation we can learn how to accept the time test, and feel no discomfort from its action, then we have succeeded in removing another anchor which is holding us down. And so it goes with all the other tests we must face.

We each of us have our strong and weak areas, and because of this each of us will face completely different tests in our journey. Early on we can face tests which may seem trivial to an outsider, but are specifically designed to clear our ego and super ego of much of its accumulated junk. As we progress we will inevitably face tests which most people would say are incredibly hard, such as the death of a close relative, a serious illness or similar unpleasant surprise.

The hallmark of how well we are doing in our yoga is how quickly we can recognise the test when it occurs (a crucial part of the battle) and how effortlessly we move past the blockade to the other side. If we can genuinely stay calm and balanced in the most serious of crises, then we are indeed progressing well. If we still lose our head, become depressed, unbalanced in any way or simply go into denial and forget everything about our spiritual focus, then we are failing the test and will need to face ourselves again in the future to pass this barrier.

The reverse of this is that overcoming a particular ordeal and passing a test is liberating and exhilarating in ways that we could

181

never imagine. This is because passing always involves identifying the test in the first place, so we always know exactly what we have left behind, and sometimes it's like dropping a ten tonne weight from our back. We realise that we have been lugging around this terrible handicap for all of our lives, but are finally rid of it and can deal with it and any of its cousins with complete confidence in the future. It is an incredibly empowering feeling and invigorating for the spirit and ones morale.

Eventually, after we have been practicing our yoga for a while, we begin to enjoy the process of each new test because we know that the ordeal comes with a stepping stone to a higher level of awareness and spiritual knowledge. The tests too, become subtler and more intricate.

Where once they may have been about our attachment to money, later on they may deal with our reluctance to handle money in case we lose ourselves in it. Later still, we may face a test where we have to accept a lot of money, say an inheritance, which on the face of it is good. But in reality the ordeal lies in how to maintain our spiritual attention when we are given enough material comfort to misdirect our focus.

One thing is certain, the flow of tapasya that the yogi faces during their journey never stops. The tests may change shape, subtlety and objective, but they will continue to occur as long as the yogi maintains the overriding desire to evolve spiritually. In fact it is pretty safe to say that a person who is meditating and facing a constant flow of personal tests is one who is ascending faster than someone who is experiencing an apparently carefree life.

Some people, however, do give up after a while, weary of the process of facing themselves, and they retreat to what appears to be an easier life focussing again on material comfort. This is a shame in so many ways, as by doing so they miss out on the most important personal goal we can pursue in any lifetime, the eternal liberation of the spirit.

Realisations

The process of self realisation is a complex one. It starts simply enough, with the awakening of our Kundalini through contact with another awakened soul, but from that point on things get a little more complicated. That initial process of self-realisation certainly opens the door to our spirituality, however when it swings open we quickly see that the lights in the next room are still switched off.

Our task from the moment we receive our realisation is to go through the different rooms of our being, switching on the lights. Every room we illuminate contains a story, from this life or a past one, which tells us what we need to do to progress to the next room. We may have to remove a particular conditioning, overcome a prejudice or forgive a long past relative. Whatever the task, we have to complete it before we can move on to the next room and the next job.

Sometimes we have a good idea of what will be facing us in a particular room, but at other times we'll be completely amazed by what we see when the lights come on. This moment is known as a realisation, a flash of understanding about our lives, environment or personality which clearly shows us what we need to do in order to progress in our spiritual ascent.

Sometimes it also takes the form of a profound insight into the human condition in general, which in turn helps us to understand ourselves and the cosmos in a deeper way. Whatever it is doesn't matter. What does matter is that we are able to recognise it and take the necessary action. Often we cannot do anything directly about these revelations at all. For instance we may realise that we have never really forgiven a long dead relative for saying something when we were younger which has made us feel guilty all of our life.

Clearly it is too late to address the situation directly now, and so instead we have to relax and let our meditation gently cleanse the problem from our subtle system over time. In other words we have to surrender the problem to our divine communication and wait for the healing process to work its way through our subtle system. This can take weeks, months, even years in cases of deep seated issues, so we have to be patient with ourselves while it happens.

It is important here to recognise the difference between a true realisation and a mere mental projection. The mind is also capable of great insight at times, and we can often be fooled into thinking that we have solved a problem just by thinking of an answer. But realisations are not simply mental insights. They are eternal truths which we actually feel deeply within our whole subtle system. We directly experience the truth of the statement, almost as if we already knew the answer and had just been reminded of it. There is no doubt, no ambivalence. The truth shines brilliantly throughout all aspects of our being; inside our heart, Chakras and mind.

This spiritual resonance marks out the real power of a realisation, as does the fact that they are intensely personal occurrences. Realisations happen exactly when we need them, and every one of us will experience realisations in their own way and related to their own requirements. These are not group shared experiences, even though their message may be a universal one. Many are so personal that they cannot even be shared with our closest friends and relatives.

One surprising fact is that they can occur anywhere, they don't necessarily happen during meditation, although they are generally associated with periods of thoughtless awareness. They will almost always be accompanied by a strong feeling of vibrations, the coolness on the hands or body which indicate a divine truth. In the ancient past these fundamental insights were delivered to solitary adepts during the course of their deeply ascetic practice in the mountains. Nowadays through the gift of Kundalini awakening our connection to the cosmos is that much stronger and so they can occur with almost miraculous regularity.

One of the main catalysts for the occurrence of these realisations is our subtle desire. In the same way that the pace of our spiritual ascent is driven by the strength of our desire to focus on our yoga meditation, so too does desire fuel our growing self awareness. Each realisation provides another milestone on the path to our full spiritual awakening, and so we need to desire that the process continues, even if we find some of the truths to be emotionally or psychologically painful.

Finally, we should remember that there is one crucially important fact that is a vital ingredient of the whole process. We must enjoy!

APPENDIX I - THE CHAKRAS

MOOLADHARA CHAKRA

Deity:	Shri Ganesha
Physical counterpart:	Pelvic Plexus, prostrate gland
Looks after:	Reproductive and excretory organs
Qualities:	Innocence, wisdom, chastity, childlike nature.
No of Petals:	Four (4)
Day:	Tuesday
Colour:	Coral Red
Element:	Carbon
Gem:	Coral
Symbol:	Clockwise Auspicious Swastika

The Mooladhara represents the beginning of time - the evolution of all things, from a single cell like the amoeba, to complex mankind. This Chakra is at the root of the whole subtle system, and so acts as the support of all the Chakras. In Sanskrit 'moola' means root and 'adhara' means the support.

Quality

The fundamental quality of this Chakra is innocence, the type of simplicity which is the basis of all righteous action. This quality is most evident in young children and babies, who will exhibit no malice or desire for personal gain at the expense of others. This is also a kind of wisdom, as when a child instinctively knows how to suck to obtain food, or cries in discomfort. Unfortunately, as we progress through childhood and life, we are beset by influences and environments which obscure the wisdom and innocence we were born with. The result is that we become tied up in a seemingly perpetual knot of complexity in our relationships and actions.

As we start meditating, however, this complexity slips away and we re-discover the joy of simplicity in our day to day lives; to take action without selfish motive, to enjoy all the aspects of life as if we were children again. This also helps us to make wiser choices in our lives and to see the innate wisdom in a correct course of action. It's easy to see just how powerful this innocent wisdom can be when we hear the truth from 'out of the mouths of babes', as illustrated by the popular fable of The Emperor's New Clothes.

Mythology

The presiding Deity (or role model) for the Mooladhara Chakra is Shri Ganesha, the eternal child with the head of an elephant. He is the archetypal innocent, and guards his Mother Kundalini (known as Gauri) and her subtle instrument with total alertness and uncompromising zeal. His symbol is the eternally auspicious swastika, which was a symbol of truth thousands of years before it was perverted by the ugliness of the World War II.

He is typically worshipped as the remover of obstacles, either in the course of awakening the Kundalini during our self-realisation process, or during our lives in general. As the eternal child Shri Ganesha bubbles with joy, enthusiasm, playfulness and love.

Gross Physical Aspect

This Chakra oversees the excretory and reproductive organs. Because of this there have been many mistaken associations in the past between sexual tantric practices and the awakening of the Kundalini. In fact this type of practice is completely against the quality of innocence which is embodied in the Mooladhara and so is doomed to failure. In certain cases it can even be dangerous with the potential to harm the natural system irreversibly.

Sex and reproduction have a vital and natural part to play in everyone's lives, however it is only when this is tempered with respect, and a balanced outlook, that we can take advantage of the power of our innate innocence. After we begin our journey of self-realisation we learn to develop this respect, and enjoy a refreshingly uncomplicated and sincere code of conduct which is the hallmark of wise and universally respected individuals.

187

Causes of problems with the Mooladhara Chakra
Left Side: Excessive sexual, tantric or occult practices.
Right Side: Excessive puritanism (e.g. a fanatical focus on the evils of the world).

Looking after the Mooladhara
A weak Mooladhara may show up as: a poor sense of direction, poor memory or sense of balance and certain other diseases or mental problems.

To help clear any problems of this Chakra we can:
Use the elements
Sit on the earth as much as possible to 'ground' our subtle system.
Soak our feet in a bowl of warm salted water whilst meditating (called 'footsoaking').
Place the right hand on or towards the ground whilst meditating.

Affirmations we can use:
Mother, please make me an innocent person.
Mother please clear my Mooladhara Chakra.
Mother, please establish innocence in me.

General Advice
Try and keep our focus on natural things such as the earth, sky or grass rather than on the gross material things which may be fighting for our attention.
Avoid too much red meat.
Meditate on the quality of innocence.
Adopt a balanced and respectful attitude towards members of the opposite sex.

Swadhishthan Chakra

Deity:	Shri Brahmadeva Shri Saraswati
Physical:	Aortic Plexus
Looks after:	Liver, kidney, spleen and pancreas.
Qualities:	Creativity, aesthetics/art, pure knowledge.
No of Petals:	Six (6)
Day:	Wednesday
Colour:	Yellow
Element:	Fire
Gem:	Amethyst
Symbol:	Star of David

The Swadhishthan Chakra is suspended like a satellite on a chord from the Nabhi Chakra, and moves around the Void area giving sustenance to the ten petals of the Void (which represent the Ten Commandments as given to Moses). When the Kundalini rises, it passes into the Nabhi Chakra first and then along the chord to enlighten the Swadhishthan and then returns to the Nabhi Chakra to continue the journey to the crown of the head.

Quality

The fundamental quality of this Chakra is that of creativity. It is here that the energy for our individual creativity is generated. After our realisation we discover that the true key to creativity lies in achieving a state of thoughtless awareness (Nirvichara Samadhi) through our meditations and from this we discover that all the beauty of the creation is reflected within us like a still and silent lake. Once we locate this pool of beauty we can become the channel for it and the pure creative instrument of the collective unconscious, without ego to distort the glory of the art. We become, as Wordsworth the poet says '*A heart that watches and receives*'!

Art which is produced in this balanced state without ego, can be said to be spiritually enhanced, i.e. it comes from the heart. If the person producing it is a 'realised soul' i.e. someone who is born with or attains complete spiritual self-knowledge – as with the classic

189

works from artists of the past such as Mozart and Michelangelo (who were born as evolved realised souls) then it can become inspired. Works of this quality are immortal, and provide joy and beauty which define a whole epoch.

The pure spirit which resides in our heart is the real reservoir of creativity, and people who think excessively or are egotistically obsessed with either fame or success will usually suffer from a weak Swadhishthan Chakra and tend to be off balance personalities. Their ambition to be superior to others or to be acclaimed by them for their talents comes from their ego, which is connected to the right side of the Swadhishthan Chakra through the right channel. Their spontaneity is lost in this ambitious and competitive effort to create. This explains why many modern artistic creations in different genres lack vitality, spirit and 'heart'.

Mythology

The presiding Deity (or role model) for the Swadhishthan Chakra is Shri Brahmadeva. He represents the ultimate

Creator, and has as his power Shri Saraswati, who is the Goddess of music and arts.

Gross Physical Aspect

One of the most important functions of this centre is that it breaks down fat particles in the abdomen to replace the grey and white cells of the brain, and so generates the energy which fuels our thinking. Excessive thinking and planning overworks this process and exhausts the centre. The Swadhishthan also looks after the liver (along with the Nabhi Centre). If the Chakra is having to cope with excessive thinking, then the other organs it is supposed to look after are neglected.

The liver has a particular importance in that it is the seat of our attention (known in the ancient Sanskrit language as Chitta). A balanced liver sustains and nourishes our attention and filters it by scanning out any external clutter. From this purified attention comes the peace and stillness that we obtain in our meditation. A liver which has been overheated by the consumption of excessive amounts of alcohol, caffeine or other stimulants can spoil our attention which will have the knock on effect of weakening our meditation and so on.

Causes of problems with the Swadhishthan Chakra

Left side: Black magic, false knowledge, drug abuse

Right side: Excessive thinking/planning, bad eating habits, ego oriented life, domination of others.

A weak Swadhishthan may show up as - irritability, difficulty meditating, inability to sit still.

To help clear any problems of the right side of this Chakra we can:

A. Use the elements

Soak the feet in a bowl of cold (or even iced) salted water at meditation.

Place an ice pack on right Swadhishthan Chakra position

B. Affirmations we can use:

Mother please take away my thoughts.

Mother, you do everything, I do nothing.

General Advice:

Right Side of the Chakra.

Place the left hand on the Chakra and right towards the photo.

Raise the left channel and bring down the right channel 108 times, with the right hand.

Use the liver diet (a diet which encourages us to eat food which is helpful to the functioning of this organ – ask for details at your local meeting).

Left Side of the Chakra

For the Left Chakra we can use warm water instead of cold, use the affirmation 'Mother, please give me the pure knowledge' and use the 3 candle treatment on the left Swadhishthan area.

NABHI CHAKRA

Deity:	Shri Vishnu (Shri Lakshmi)/Shri Shesha
Physical:	Solar Plexus
Looks after:	Stomach, intestines, spleen, pancreas, liver.
Qualities:	Satisfaction, domestic well-being, peace and generosity.
No of Petals:	Ten (10)
Day:	Thursday
Colour:	Green
Element:	Water
Gem:	Emerald
Symbol:	Yin/Yang

The evolutionary growth of humankind mirrors the ascending Chakras of our subtle system, and our corresponding spiritual growth path. The Nabhi Chakra represents the evolutionary point when man's shelter became 'home'; when the family unit became a source of satisfaction in itself rather than just a mere channel for reproduction. This domestic satisfaction translates into the kind of satisfaction that we feel with life in general after our spiritual awakening through self-realisation. Once we achieve this state of well-being, we can move on to search for more enlightening and spiritual truths.

Quality

Satisfaction is a key word for the Nabhi Chakra. Some 'hot livered' people are naturally irritable. For them life without worry is an impossibility and they will express their discontent at the slightest excuse. When our spirit manifests we can put things into their true perspective, and worry becomes an unusual occurrence. Only in the peace of thoughtlessness can we be content. We realise that the spirit is not concerned with passing trends and fashions, a button missing here or there. The affirmation for the Nabhi Chakra is '*In my spirit I am satisfied*'.

The Nabhi is the centre of welfare, both physical and financial. Prosperity is a necessary step in evolution, and money is a valid medium of exchange in order to obtain the essential needs and desires of man. However, sometimes we get lost and our desire for basic needs turns into a cycle of insatiable desire for things in general – the start of a materialist existence.

After our realisation we understand that while there is no harm in being wealthy, we do not need to focus all of our attention on the pursuit of money. That money is simply a commodity which should flow responsibly into and out of our possession like food and water. In this way we lose our selfishness and learn generosity, the key to an open heart.

Another key aspect of this Chakra is the elevating power of the balanced household. The respect which exists between family members is the foundation on which modern civilisation has been built, and from this relationship comes the decency and generosity by which humankind is judged. After our realisation we begin to understand more about the place of the family in our life, and in turn develop a more positive attitude in all of our relationships. We learn that marriage and relationships offer much more than just material stability, and in fact can provide a spiritual component which adds profound peace to our lives.

Mythology
The presiding deity (or role model) of the centre is Shri Vishnu, the Preserver. He it is who sustains our Dharma – our righteous behaviour and lifestyle - and leads us in our evolution. The power of the Nabhi Chakra rests with Shri Lakshmi, from whom we obtain our physical and material well-being (Kshema). She it is also who is the source of the peace which we get from our spiritual awakening and through our meditation.

Gross Physical Aspect
This centre governs the workings of the stomach area. If the functioning of the stomach becomes disturbed, then the process of digestion and assimilation of food is affected and we will fail to receive proper nourishment. It is important, therefore that we eat

193

balanced meals with proper respect for the process. The Nabhi Chakra is also responsible for the liver, and the importance of this organ for our meditation and attention cannot be stressed too much. It is very important to take particular care of the liver (which is prone to overheating through improper diet or stimulants) and to ensure that we do not exhaust it too much through our thinking and planning.

Causes of problems with the Nabhi Chakra

Left side: Excessive worrying about household affairs.

Right side: Excessive gluttony or attention to food, drug and alcohol abuse, fanaticism of any kind, money problems.

In general a weakened Nabhi may be indicated by – excessive worrying, fanaticism or asceticism, stomach problems.

To help clear any problems of the Chakra we can:

A. Use the elements

Footsoaking

Candle treatment of the stomach area

Place an ice pack on liver area.

B. Affirmations we can use:

Mother please make me a generous person

Mother, in my spirit I am satisfied.

General Advice:

Try not to complain too much about your life.

Avoid fatty foods and excessive dairy products if you suffer from problems with the right Nabhi.

Eat a nourishing and balanced diet, including fresh fruit and vegetables.

Avoid miserliness and try to be satisfied with what you have.

Watch/witness any anger that arises in you and become detached from the cause and effect.

Use the liver diet as necessary.

Moderate your intake of stimulants including coffee and alcohol.

HEART (ANAHAT) CHAKRA

Deity: Shri Shiva Shri Parvati, Shri Jagadambe, Shri Rama Shri Sita
Physical: Cardiac Plexus, heart organ, sternum.
Looks after: Heartbeat, breathing, chest area.
Qualities: Security, joy, love, auspiciousness, duty and compassion.
No of Petals: Twelve (12)
Day: Friday
Colour: Dark Red
Element: Air
Gem: Ruby
Symbol: Flame

The newborn baby is pure spirit, with no ego, conditionings or mind at work. This purely spiritual being finds solace immediately in its mother, joined by an innate love that responds to the closeness and warmth of its mother's love and spirit. It is a true bonding in every way.

Quality

The Heart Chakra is the home of the self, the spirit, the Atma. This spirit can only manifest when our heart is open and clean, at which point we feel the eternal joy of the creation and the meaning and purpose of our place in it. We clean our heart through our pure Desire, and through purifying our attention in meditation.

But above all it is love, pure love which enlightens all, which is the real quality of the Heart Chakra. Before our realisation we rarely love for love's sake. Instead we mistake feelings of love with physical attraction, infatuation and selfishness. Pure love has no motive, it emanates from the spirit and not from the body or mind. Like the tree which gives shade it has no need of reward.

Love also flows through all parts of life, through society and the world. Love is God, we say, and God is love, because in real Love there is no I or you, just the merging of the spirit.

Security is also another aspect of this Chakra. As we meditate we begin to benefit from a growing strength as our heart becomes nourished with love. And as we become 'lion hearted' we become physically stronger, more able to withstand disease and illness. We also start to benefit from closer relationships with our parents and partners as we start to treat them with reverence and affection.

In all aspects of our lives, the Heart Chakra plays a vital role. Without a strong heart we cannot make the important decisions necessary to further our growth as a person. Without an open heart we cannot recognise the beauty and majesty of God and nature. Without a loving heart we cannot give to others, instead we continue to demand and grab everything we can in an insecure fervour of misunderstanding. Without love and a good heart there can be no peace, and without peace there can be no joy in our lives.

Mythology

The presiding deity (or role model) of the left Heart Chakra is Shri Shiva (controlling our very existence as the witness of all), of the right Shri Rama and of the centre Heart Shri Jagadambe, the Mother of the Universe. Each role model offers us private guidance as to the path we need to tread to fulfil the promise of our birth.

Gross Physical Aspect

The heart is the pump of the body and so any physical or mental excess can strain the centre with potentially drastic results. The Heart is the home of our individual spirit and so we must respect its importance in our lives in every way. Excessive thinking or athleticism are also not good for the proper functioning of this Chakra.

Causes of problems with the Heart Chakra

Left side: Lack of faith, neglect of the spirit, excessive vulgarity and extreme physical/mental activity, problems with maternal relationships.

Right side: Arrogance, aggressive behaviour, problems with the fraternal/masculine relationship.

Centre: Insecurity, fear, miserliness.

In general a weak Heart may be indicated by – overly ascetic tendencies, insecurity or extreme physical activity resulting in frail health, neuroses or allergies.

To help clear any problems of the Chakra we can:
A. Use the elements.
Controlled deep breathing exercises for the centre heart.
Candle treatment of the left or centre heart areas.

B. Affirmations we can use:
Mother, please make me a fearless person.
Mother, I am the spirit, not this body, ego or mind.

General Advice:
Centre: Say to yourself *'Jagadambe'* quietly 12 times, breathe in, hold the breath and then let it out - three times.
Recite the 23rd Psalm from The Bible or read the Indian text, The Devi Mahatmyam.

Left: Keep your attention on the spirit residing in your Heart.
Put the right hand on the left heart centre and hold the left hand out towards the photograph and candle.

Right: Avoid taking on too much responsibility. Delegate!
Raise and move the left side into the right 108 times during your meditation.
Live within the boundaries of good conduct in family and general life. This is Dharma!

VISHUDDHI CHAKRA

Deity:	Shri Krishna Shri Radha, Shri Vishnumaya, Shri Yeshoda
Physical:	Cervical Plexus (thyroid)
Looks after:	Neck, arms, face, tongue, mouth, nose, teeth
Qualities:	Diplomacy, collectivity, detachment, fun, self respect, brother/sister relationship.
No of Petals:	Sixteen (16)
Day:	Saturday
Colour:	Blue/Grey
Element:	Ether
Gem:	Sapphire
Symbol:	Timewheel

The Vishuddhi Chakra represents the point at which mankind finally moved away from the animal kingdom and lifted its head up to the stars. This transition to Homo Erectus was pivotal in the formation of society and civilisation, and hence it is fitting that the Vishuddhi should have such a powerful influence on all aspects of communication and community.

Quality

Detachment and a sense of perspective are important features of the Vishuddhi Chakra. The ability to determine what is really important in our lives, and realise that problems are usually simply a creation of our own conditionings and fears. As a result we become stronger and more able to handle things which at first glance appear to be traumatic but in fact are nothing more than events we must pass through on our way through life.

Existence is about evolution through challenge, whether it be the law of the jungle or the ways of the world .After our realisation we learn how to become comfortable with this fact.

The Vishuddhi also embodies those qualities which govern our relationship with others. Lack of respect for others and for ourselves (i.e. guilt) are important and can hinder our progress towards the spirit. Through our meditation we learn to stop feeling guilty, face up to our weaknesses and do something positive about them. The affirmation for the left Vishuddhi is '*I am not guilty*'.

It is this centre also which governs our collectivity, how we relate to one another and to the Universe as a whole. As we progress in our meditations we will find that we become more compassionate towards others and more able to give where giving is due. The Hamsa Chakra, which is located on the bridge of the nose, is also a part of the Vishuddhi, and gives us that all important sense of discrimination and discretion to help us determine the right course of action in our everyday lives.

Mythology

The presiding Deity (or role model) for the Vishuddhi Chakra is Shri Krishna. He represents God in His aspect as the detached yogi. With complete detachment he watches the Play (or Leela) of life and death, the cosmic drama. He is also the Master of Yoga, and the guide who leads us on towards oneness with the spirit and the Universe.

Gross Physical Aspect

This Chakra looks after the throat, mouth, face, teeth and so on. In order to avoid problems with this Chakra we should take proper care of our teeth, avoid pollutants such as tobacco which can damage the throat and generally take extra precautions in extreme climates. We should try and respect everything we do in our communication with others; talk sweetly, avoid ugly gestures and grimaces and try to demonstrate our open heart through our communication. The Vishuddhi Chakra is also very important for our awareness of Vibrations, because the nerves which register the physical sensation of coolness pass through this centre.

Causes of problems with the Vishuddhi Chakra

Left Side: Guilt, immorality, foul speech, sarcasm, lack of self respect.

Right Side: Disrespect for others, aggression, domination

Centre: Lack of detachment or collectivity.

In general a weak Vishuddhi may show up as – excessive colds or sore throats, coughing or symptoms with the ears or nose. If we feel guilty we can experience sore or tense shoulders and find ourselves talking harshly for no reason.

To help clear any problems of this Chakra we can:
Use the elements.

Candle treatment around the left and centre throat area.

Nasal breathing exercises (commonly used in Bastrika – Hatha Yoga)

Affirmations we can use:
Mother, please make me part and parcel of the whole.
Mother, I am not guilty of anything at all (for the left side).

General Advice
Always protect the throat against the cold weather with a scarf or similar.

Use a salt water gargle for sore throats if necessary.

Brush the teeth regularly.

Drops of oil in the ears or throat, or taking honey, can also help problems.

Do not speak sarcastically or harshly to others. Also if possible avoid arguments, or even excessive conversation.

Massage your neck and shoulders with any vitamin enriched oil if there is pain.

AGNYA CHAKRA

Deity:	Lord Jesus Christ Mother Mary, Shri Buddha, Shri Mahavira.
Physical:	Optic Chiasma (pineal/pituitary)
Looks after:	Sight, hearing, thought, memories, I-ness.
Qualities:	Forgiveness, resurrection, humility.
No of Petals:	Two (2)
Day:	Sunday
Colour:	White
Element:	Light
Gem:	Diamond
Symbol:	The Cross

The Agnya Chakra is situated in the centre of the area of the brain. It acts as the gateway to the Sahasrara Chakra by stopping the rise of the Kundalini if there are any impurities in the mind. When the Kundalini does pass through this Chakra, however, our thought waves elongate so that the space between any two thoughts grows wider. This space is silence, and as the petals of the Chakra open, the silence spreads outwards, pushing our thoughts to the periphery of our awareness. This is where the state of 'thoughtless awareness' originates. In this state we can actually feel the profound peace, the stillness, which is at the heart of creation.

Quality

The primary quality of the Agnya Chakra is forgiveness, for without this forbearance we cannot progress beyond our ego and become the spirit. The ego is a creature of action. It thrives on doing - on punishing for a wrong, on effecting a change, on obtaining a desire. By practising forbearance, we slow down the fuel of the ego, we force the ego to wait. By so doing our spirit then has the time to shine through in our action, and the true course becomes manifest. Once we see that anger is self-destructive, that it is we who suffer as a result of this emotion, then it becomes easier to forgive.

The Agnya also sits at the crucial fulcrum of our thinking engine, the mind. The mind is divided into ego and super ego, two aspects that ultimately isolate us from our spirit. We don't have to destroy our ego in order to evolve – it is very useful, for without it we would not be able to act at all – but we need to bring it into a balanced relationship within our subtle system. In this way the spirit can start to shine in our personality and the Kundalini can pass through into the Sahasrara Chakra and complete our yoga, our union.

We can never fight our ego – fighting requires action, the action is ego, therefore ego fights ego! But we can bring it into balance by watching it, by using humour, by allowing the power of our heart to counterbalance its excesses. In similar ways our super ego, which reflects the conditionings which come from our past relationships and environment, has to be brought into balance with the system otherwise we become suffocated by a judgmental and emotional turmoil within our minds. We can do this if we stop indulging in our past, and start to enjoy the joys of the present moment more.

Mythology

The presiding Deity (or role model) of the left Agnya Chakra is Shri Mahavira, of the right, Shri Buddha and the centre is Shri Jesus. All of these great incarnations preached the fundamental truths of forgiveness, balanced gentle thought and action and the ultimate goal of attaining the eternal spirit. The spirit is beyond thought, beyond Karma, beyond sin.

Gross Physical Aspect

Amongst other things, the Agnya Chakra governs our sight. We should therefore respect the eyes as a gift with which the beauty of the Divine creation is revealed to us. We should not waste or abuse that gift. We should try and avoid squandering our vision and attention on the gross aspects of the material world and deliberately encourage ourselves to take time out to enjoy the natural beauty of things like the sky, trees or grass, or even look at a naked flame as a means of cleansing this centre.

202

Causes of problems with the Agnya Chakra:
    Left Side: Self pity, living in the past, harm to self.
    Right Side: Worries, aggression, egoism, harm to others.
    Centre: Roving eyes, inappropriate relationships.

In general a weak Agnya may show up as: Headaches, shoulder pain or problems with the memory.

To help clear any problems of this Chakra we can:
    A. Use the elements
    Look at a naked flame to clear the centre.
    In severe cases use camphor treatment on the back of the head for back/left Agnya.
    Look at Nature, smell flowers, bathe centre in sunlight.

    Right side problem: Realise that you are not the doer (say 'I am not the doer of anything'). Raise the left side energy into the right side 108 times during meditation.
    Left Side problem: Raise the right side energy into the left.

    B. Affirmations we can use:
    Mother, I forgive everyone including myself.
    Mother You do everything I do nothing.
    Mother, please forgive me for anything I may have done against my spirit.

General Advice

    For the left/back Agnya, do not dwell in the past. Stop indulging and start living for the moment.
    Front Agnya: Let go of futuristic and fanatical tendencies.
    Stop all alternative meditative activities specifically involving the Agnya – i.e. visualisation, hypnosis, clairvoyance.
    In general forgive everyone without discrimination, from the heart and sincerely.

Sahasrara Chakra

Deity:	Shri Kalki, Shri Adi Shakti
Physical:	Limbic system
Looks after:	Vibrations, cool breeze, yoga.
Qualities:	Collective consciousness, integration, silence.
No of Petals:	One thousand (1000)
Day:	Monday
Colour:	Multicolour – all the colours
Element:	All the elements
Gem:	Pearl
Symbol:	The Bandhan

Our complete subtle instrument is integrated in the Sahasrara Chakra. Each Chakra has its own place here and this is where the Deities have their seats within the Virata – the Cosmic Body.

Quality

At the point of the Sahasrara we go beyond the relative, to the absolute. Beyond time, space or energy and into the absolute realisation of heaven on earth. This is a place far beyond our wildest imaginings, so much more than our words can even seek to imply. This is our ultimate destination, stretching to infinity. When the Kundalini reaches the Sahasrara, the 1000 petals of the Chakra open like a Lotus and enlightenment takes place (Samadhi). We may experience a powerful pulsation in the crown of the head, followed by a melting sensation and a subtle stream of cool vibrations flowing from the crown of the head.

Vibratory awareness begins at this point. As the Kundalini unites our individual consciousness to the universal consciousness (the Atma to the Paramatma), we are suddenly tuned in to the universal wavelength of vibrations. These vibrations pervade the cosmos, but before realisation, while we are still in the egg form, we know nothing of them. When the Kundalini breaks the shell of the egg, we emerge into God's Kingdom, the realm of supreme Collective Consciousness. At this point we are singing the song of the Divine

204

and the vibrations start playing through the instrument that we have become.

As human awareness is united to the Divine in this manner, we move into the subtlest level of communication, into Collective Consciousness. In becoming vehicles for that Universal power we become one with all others. We learn to appreciate the real depth and beauty of another person in vibrations. The beauty of art and nature now manifests itself as vibrations. Just ask any question and a positive or negative reply will manifest as a flow of cool or warm vibrations. It is conversation at its most sublime.

But, as it says in the Bhagvad Gita, a doubting mind cannot ascend.

But the man who is ignorant, who has no faith, who is of a doubting nature, perishes. For the doubting soul, there is neither this world nor the world beyond nor any happiness. We must have a positive basis for life, an unwavering faith to discover the truth which stands the test of life. The Bhagavad Gita IV:40

Mythology

The presiding Deity (or role model) of the Sahasrara Chakra is Shri Kalki. With his eleven destructive powers (Ekadesha Rudra) he is the final, most awesome incarnation of Shri Vishnu. He is the rider of the apocalypse whose only objective is the end of evil. He is the last judgement, and the judgement is all around and within us . We rise or fall according to our Kundalini. It is She who will give us all the chance to recognise the Truth. It is only through vibratory awareness that we can truly discriminate between that which is true, and that which is false.

Shri Mataji, as the source of this Mahayoga, also has Her place in the Sahasrara. Through Her grace, our Kundalini is awakened, our eternal spirit is enlightened and we begin to feel the vibrations. Because of Her, we also can awaken the Kundalini of others after our own awakening. We can give realisation to others, we can cure sickness and we can share the message of Divine Love with the entire world.

She describes it thus:

"The limited capacity of the brain becomes unlimited in its capacity to realise God. If you are the sun and the sunlight, if you are the moon and the moonlight, where is the duality? Only when there is separation is there duality and because of that separation you feel attachment.... a distance between you and yours - that's why you get attached to it. Everything is we, who is the other? When the brain has lost its identity, the so called limited brain becomes the unlimited Spirit."

Causes of problems with the Sahasrara Chakra
Atheism, Doubt in God, anti-God activities.

To help clear any problems of this Chakra we can use:
Affirmations.
Mother, please give me my self-realisation.
Mother please establish my self-realisation.

General Advice
Massage the top of the head with even hand pressure, move the scalp to and fro many times until any pressure on the head reduces.

Using cupped hands massage the sides of the head.

Massage the skin on the crown (top) of the head in a clockwise direction 7 times and ask for self-realisation.

RAISING KUNDALINI AND THE BANDHAN

Raising our Kundalini and putting ourselves in Bandhan is an important step in readying ourselves for meditation or workshop. We use these simple techniques to help bring our system into balance and to place ourselves into a protective state both before and after meditation.

Figs 1 – 4

It is our Kundalini energy, rising up the spine, which takes our attention higher into the state of thoughtless awareness. This exercise helps to strengthen, steady and establish the attention in the highest energy centre, the Sahasrara Chakra.

Raising our own Kundalini, at the beginning and end of every meditation, helps to settle our subtle system into a more balanced state. Begin with the left hand at the front at the level of the abdomen, palm facing towards the body. While rotating the right hand around the left hand, move the left hand up the front of the body and over the head and tie a knot at the top to symbolically keep our attention up there. Use this movement three times and on the third time tie three knots over the top of your head.

Figs. 5 – 6

A simple exercise to protect our subtle body, and preserve our state of meditation, is to put on a bandhan. This exercise should be done before and after meditation, just after raising the Kundalini (as above).

Hold the left hand out (palm upwards) at the level of the waist, with the fingers pointing towards the photograph of Shri Mataji. Using the right hand, trace an arc over the head, starting at the level of the left hip, over the top to the right hip and then back again to the left hip. This movement should be done seven times (once for every Chakra in the subtle system).

Appendix C
Experience Self-Realisation

You can experience the initial process of self-realisation right here and now if you wish. It is simple to achieve and takes only a few minutes of your time.

First, if you have a candle, place it on an empty table or other suitable surface and light it. For a more intense experience place this book upright on the table so that you can also see the photo of Shri Mataji on the back cover.

Now remove your shoes and sit down comfortably on a chair or the floor, with your back straight and your hands resting on your lap with the palms upwards.

Gaze at the candle or the photo for a few moments to enter into a peaceful state and then close your eyes in order to take your attention inside. Ignore any sounds going on around you and just sit silently for a minute or so. You can take three deep breaths if that helps to settle your attention, but don't worry about whether you're doing anything properly, just relax.

Now say silently to yourself, from the heart and with full desire – "Mother, please give me my self-realisation." Say this three times, slowly and with conviction.

At this point you can just sit silently and try not to think of anything, to allow the Kundalini time to begin to rise up the spine. Ignore any sensations such as heat or cool, tingling or twinges and just sit with a calm and steady attention.

You are now entering into a state of meditation, and should be experiencing a state of alert, but peaceful consciousness; thoughtless awareness. You may also be experiencing a sensation of coolness, like a very faint breeze on your hands or coming from the top of your head. After a while you can check this by holding your right or left hand six inches above the head, but you shouldn't let it distract you from the zone of peace you are experiencing.

There might be a little warmth as the Kundalini cleanses the Chakras, or tingling as they clear and open, but again these are just symptoms of your subtle spiritual system coming to life and you should not focus on them or worry about these sensations.

It may be that you are unable to feel anything from this process of self-realisation, but don't worry. This could be because one or more of your Chakras is blocked and needs extra cleansing. For example heavy smokers may not feel any coolness as their Vishuddhi Chakra may be a little constricted at first.

It's nothing to worry about, and eventually the sensations will fade away. You can also help the process along by saying silently to yourself, '*I forgive everyone for everything, and I forgive myself*' and by affirming with conviction '*Mother, I am not guilty of anything at all*'.

There is no need to chant these repetitively, just say them a few times to help clear the affected Chakras. We often unconsciously carry around a large amount of accumulated guilt which can impede the flow of spiritual energy and make it difficult for us to experience the full beauty of a meditation. Patience and a strong desire will pay dividends in these cases.

Now, after the end of the meditation, see if you are feeling relaxed and if your thoughts have slowed down or gradually disappeared. This is the first stage of meditation - thoughtless awareness - where you are fully alert but without any thoughts, in a state of pure and peaceful consciousness.

That is the process of self-realisation. Deceptively simple and yet infinitely profound, it is the wisdom of the ages and the secret of reality wrapped up in a single moment of peace and serenity. Enjoy.

Appendix D – Liver Diet

First of all it needs to be said that having a liver which needs Sahaj treatment does not necessarily indicate wrong doing or physical illness. Many of our problems with this organ are caused simply by living in the fast moving and inherently hostile modern environment. Fast food, a stressful job and even things like planning complex holidays can add to the work the liver has to do. The key is in recognising the signs and taking remedial action so that we stay in balance and our meditation does not suffer.

If you suddenly feel that your meditations are not going so well, for example that you are thinking too much, you can do a simple test. Try meditating for one day with an ice pack placed over the area of the liver (right hand side of the body, bottom of the rib cage). If your meditation improves, this is an indication that the source of the problem may well be the liver.

If the problem persists or becomes more severe, then you should seriously consider using the liver diet to correct things. Try it for seven to ten days, at the end of that time you should be able to notice a marked difference in your meditations and overall state of balance.

The Diet

There are two basic things to remember about the Liver Diet – first, cooling foods help the liver function properly, and second, heating foods impede the liver's natural processes. Obviously we want to eat cooling foods in order to help our system work at its best. There are no surprising aspects to this diet, it basically just involves eating sensibly - good food, well prepared.

Cooling Foods. Recommended:
★ Sugar. Shri Mataji has said that sugar is the food of the liver. This is cane sugar, not beet. Tate & Lyle sugar, for example, is cane, the others are almost always beet. There is also a type of sugar

known as sugar candy or rock sugar, which is available from most Indian shops – its use is described under Black Kokum below.

★ White Rice. White rice is very cooling for the liver.

★ Yoghurt. This is probably the most effective coolant. However it should not be eaten in a cold climate or time of year such as winter/spring.

★ Ginger. Ginger in almost any form is good for the liver. In particular we can take some in the morning in a spoon mixed with sugar, followed by a glass of water.

★ Crystallised ginger is also very good. This mixture should not, however, be taken in very hot climates or hot times of the year such as summer.

★ Fruit. Generally most fruit is good for the Nabhi Chakra and therefore the liver. In particular grapes are good, and grape juice in its pure form is also very beneficial.

★ Vegetables & Salads etc. All are very good for the liver in general. Radishes in particular (and their leaves) can be taken and boiled with sugar candy and drunk as a beverage.

★ Chana. Known also as chick peas. Can be made into dhal or soup. These chick peas are very good for the whole Nabhi Chakra.

★ Black Kokum. This is a type of fruit which can be bought from most Indian stores. They look like prunes but be warned, they are not sweet! The best way to use them is to make a drink out of them by pouring boiling water over a small handful in a jug, with about the same quantity of sugar candy. The mixture should then be left overnight and the juice drunk the next day as a normal beverage in place of tea or coffee.

Heating Foods. To be avoided:

★ Alcohol. Alcohol has a detrimental effect on the liver and should be avoided if possible during the diet phase.

★ Fried, fatty or oily foods.

★ Heavy (e.g. red) meat.

★ Butter and cream/ice cream. Also chocolate!

★ Very spicy foods.

★ Fish

★ Processed white bread

★ Coffee (especially if strong) and non China tea.

Not advisable. Try to avoid or consume only in moderation:
★ Cheese and most dairy products.
★ Too much milk
★ Too much salt.

OK in small amounts:
★ Chicken.
★ Unprocessed whole grain bread

A typical meal using this special liver diet then could be a simple chicken and white rice dish (without any rich sauces or spices), with salad and fruit or yoghurt to follow. In general it is simply advisable to cut out all the harmful foods during the diet period and try and eat the beneficial foods, whilst paying special attention to our liver in our meditation. We can use the ice pack treatment also during this time.

Appendix E – Sahaja Yoga Websites Worldwide

Sahaja Yoga International - http://www.sahajayoga.org/

Argentina	– www.sahajayoga.org.ar/
Australia	– www.freemeditation.com/
Austria	– www.yoga.or.at
Belgium	– www.sahajayoga.be
Benin	– www.sahajayogabenin.com
Brazil	– www.sahajayoga.org.br
Bulgaria	– www.infotel.bg/~shanti
Canada	– www.sahajayoga.ca
Colombia	– www.sahajacolombia.org.co
Cote d'Ivoire	– www.ci.sahaja-yoga.net/
Croatia	– www.sahajayogacroatia.org
Czech Rep.	– www.nirmala.cz
Denmark	– www.sahajayoga.dk
Estonia	– www.sahadzajooga.ee/
Finland	– www.jooga.org
France	– www.sahajayoga.asso.fr
Germany	– www.sahaja-yoga.de/home.htm
Greece	– www.sahajayogahellas.org
Hong Kong	– www.sahajayoga.org.hk
Hungary	– www.sahajajoga.hu
India	– www.sahajayoga.in/
Ireland (Eire)	– www.irelandyoga.org
Israel	– www.sahajayoga.org.il
Italy	– www.sahajayoga.it

Japan	– www.t3.rim.or.jp/~hitoshii
Lithuania	– www.sahadzajoga.lt
Luxembourg	– http://home.pi.be/~pin25815/lux
Malaysia	– www.sahajmalaysia.org
Netherlands	– www.sahajayoga.nl/
New Zealand	– http://homepages.ihug.co.nz/~sahaj_nz
Nigeria	– www.sahajayoganigeria.org
Norway	– www.synorge.net
Poland	– www.sahajayoga.pl
Romania	– www.sahajayoga.ro
Russia	– www.sahajayoga.ru
Saudi Arabia	– www.sahajayoga-arabia.com
Singapore	– http://home2.pacific.net.sg/~kulkar
Slovakia	– www.sahajayoga.sk
Slovenia	– www.jogaslovenija.org
South Africa	– www.sahajayoga.co.za
Spain	– www.sahajayoga.es
Sweden	– www.meditationforalla.nu
Switzerland	– www.sahajayoga.ch
Taiwan	– www.sahajayoga-tw.com
Thailand	– www.thai.net/sahajayoga
Trinidad &T.	– http://sahajayogatt.netfirms.com/
Turkey	– www.sahajayogaturkey.f2s.com
Ukraine	– www.sahajayoga.org.ua
UAE	– www.sahajayogauae.com
UK	– www.sahajayoga.org.uk
USA	– www.sahajayoga.org/usa/

Notes

[i] Professor Donald Hoffman, cognitive scientist, University of California, *New York Times*, January 4th 2005.

[ii] Unattributed, but according to Simpson's Contemporary Quotations, the quote was recalled on his death – 18th April 1955.

[iii] Erwin Schroedinger, *My View Of The World*, 1961.

[iv] Professor Michael Behe, *Darwin's Black Box: The Biochemical Challenge to Evolution*, 1998.

[v] Letter to John Hamilton Reynolds, February 1818.

[vi] Jung, C. G. (1923). *Psychological Types*. New York, Harcourt, Brace and Company (p. 628)

[vii] Linda J. Harrison, Ramesh Manocha, and Katya Rubia, *Sahaja Yoga Meditation as a Family Treatment Programme for Children with Attention Deficit-Hyperactivity Disorder*, Clinical Child Psychology and Psychiatry, *Oct 2004*

[viii] Dr Ramesh Manocha, *Researching Meditation*, Diversity, Vol 2, No 5, June 2001.

[ix] Dr Guy B Marks, *Sahaja Yoga in the management of moderate to severe asthma…*, Thorax, February 2002, Vol 57, No 2, pp 110-115, http://www.nih.gov/news/NIH-Record/08_25_98/briefs.htm.

CPSIA information can be obtained at www.ICGtesting.com
Printed in the USA
LVOW041531250712

291532LV00002B/37/A